RECOMMENDED READINGS IN LITERATURE

ANNOTATED EDITION

KINDERGARTEN THROUGH GRADE EIGHT

Prepared by the
Language Arts and Foreign Languages Unit
and the
Bureau of Publications
California State Department of Education

Publishing Information

This annotated version of *Recommended Readings in Literature* was
prepared by the Department of Education's Language Arts and Foreign
Languages Unit, working with an advisory committee and members of the
California Reading Association (see Acknowledgments). The Department
published an unannotated version of *Recommended Readings* in 1986.
This new document was edited for publication by Mirko Strazicich of the
Bureau of Publications, working cooperatively with Leonard Hull of the
Language Arts and Foreign Languages Unit. It was prepared for photo-
offset production by the staff of the Bureau of Publications, with artwork
and layout design by Cheryl Shawver McDonald and typesetting by Anna
Boyd and Leatrice Shimabukuro.

The document was published by the California State Department of
Education, 721 Capitol Mall, Sacramento, California (mailing address:
P.O. Box 944272, Sacramento, CA 94244-2720). It was printed by the
Office of State Printing and distributed under the provisions of the
Library Distribution Act and *Government Code* Section 11096.

Copies of this publication are available for $4.50 each, plus sales tax for
California residents, from the Bureau of Publications Sales, California
State Department of Education, P.O. Box 271, Sacramento, CA 95802-
0271 (telephone: 916-445-1260). An order form is provided on page 128 of
this publication.

A list of other publications available from the Department of Education
may be found on page 126 of this publication.

ISBN 0-8011-0745-8

Credits

The annotations in the margins of this document were extrapolated
from *Becoming a Nation of Readers: The Report of the Commission on
Reading* (published by the National Institute of Education, U.S. Department of Education, 1984) and *What Works: Research About Teaching and
Learning* (published by the U.S. Department of Education, 1986).

Contents

FOREWORD

"Once upon a time" is a phrase that stirs excitement in the hearts of children. They immediately know that they are going to be treated to a story—a story that will entertain them, a story that will inform them about their world, and a story that will tickle their imaginations. These experiences may be shared with children at home, in the classroom, and in the library. Such experiences may include the reading of a fairy tale, such as *Three Billy Goats Gruff* for the younger children; a modern fantasy, such as *Charlotte's Web* for the middle grade students; or a Shakespearean play for the older students.

Literature is for all children, regardless of their ages or grade levels. Reading should begin in the home and progress into a lifelong experience. Literature carries messages about life that are essential to complete a child's proper growth and development. Rather than being fragmented bits and pieces that lack "story structure," these literary works need to be complete stories that young readers will grasp and remember.

I am recommending the books that are listed in this document as examples of good literature for children. The more than 1,000 listed titles represent the advisory committee members' selections of children's classics, modern-day classics, and storybooks for recreational reading. As you plan your literature program, you should find this new edition even more useful than was the original edition, because all the title entries are annotated.

Bill Honig

Superintendent of Public Instruction

PREFACE

This publication, *Recommended Readings in Literature,* was compiled by teachers, administrators, curriculum planners, and librarians located throughout California to (1) encourage students to read and to view reading as a worthwhile activity; (2) help local curriculum planners select books for their reading programs; and (3) stimulate educators at the local level to evaluate their literature programs and change or improve them, if necessary.

To ensure that *Recommended Readings in Literature* would help educators review their literature programs and encourage students to read, the compilers formed two working groups—one to formulate a list of readings and another to review and refine the list. Working together for over a year, the groups reviewed over 2,000 titles. And after many meetings, telephone calls, and exchanges of letters, the members agreed on the 1,010 titles listed in this document. These titles represent classical as well as contemporary works of fiction, nonfiction, poetry, and drama. The list also includes works that students whose primary language is other than English will enjoy.

We give special recognition to Leonard Hull, Consultant in the Language Arts and Foreign Languages Unit. Because of his untiring efforts and patience, *Recommended Readings in Literature* has become a reality. We are grateful to the educators whose names appear in the Acknowledgments for developing and producing a document that represents such a wide variety of titles in children's literature—titles that educators can recommend and students can read with pleasure.

We are pleased to present this edition of *Recommended Readings in Literature, Kindergarten Through Grade Eight.* Since the original edition was published two years ago, we have received numerous suggestions for improving the lists. These ideas and comments led to the development of this updated document. You will note that we have added an annotation to each title entry to further aid you when you use the lists to choose books for your literature program.

JAMES R. SMITH
Deputy Superintendent
Curriculum and
Instructional Leadership

FRANCIE ALEXANDER
Director
Curriculum, Instruction, and
Assessment Division

TOMAS LOPEZ
Manager
Office of Humanities
Curriculum Services

Acknowledgments

his book list was prepared with the help of an advisory committee composed of school administrators, curriculum planners and consultants, college professors, teachers, and librarians. Superintendent Bill Honig and members of his staff are most grateful for the efforts and contributions of the advisory committee members and also the educators and librarians who served on field review groups that responded to the drafts of this document. The members of the advisory committee included the following:

Alma Flor Ada, Professor, University of San Francisco
Joan Mayhew Beales, Teacher, Reed Elementary School, Tiburon
Donna Bessant, District Librarian, Monterey Peninsula Unified School District
Yetive Bradley, Principal, Grass Valley Elementary School, Oakland
Patricia Brose,* Professor, California State University, Chico
Jacqueline Chaparro, English/Language Arts Coordinator, Office of the San Diego County Superintendent of Schools
Jesus Cortez, Director of Bilingual Education, California State University, Chico
Ann Emanuels, Teacher, Deterding Elementary School, Carmichael
Ruth Gibbs, Consultant, South Bay Writing Project
Josephine Gusman, Teacher, Newcomer Center, Sacramento
Walter Loban, Professor Emeritus, University of California, Berkeley
Joan Macon, Teacher, Wakeham Elementary School, Garden Grove
Zhita Rea,* Library Consultant, Office of the Los Angeles County Superintendent of Schools
Virginia Reid, Teacher (retired), University of California, Berkeley Extension School
Alice Scofield, Professor, San Jose State University
Carol Tateishi, Teacher, Ross Elementary School
Eleanor Thonis, District Psychologist, Wheatland Elementary School District
Ellis Vance, District Coordinator, Clovis Unified School District

Liaison from the Model Curriculum Guide Committee: William H. Thomas, Language Curriculum Specialist, Mt. Diablo Unified School District

Compiler: Leonard Hull, Consultant (retired), Language Arts and Foreign Languages Unit, State Department of Education

Computer programmer for the project: Linda Vocal, State Department of Education

State Department of Education staff support was provided by the following consultants:

Gene Bradford, Language Arts and Foreign Languages Unit
Kate Farrell, Zellerbach Family Fund Consultant attached to the Language Arts and Foreign Languages Unit
Eva Fong, External Affairs Office
Mae Gundlach, Language Arts and Foreign Languages Unit
Shirley Hazlett, Language Arts and Foreign Languages Unit
Adele Martinez, Language Arts and Foreign Languages Unit
Terry Martinez, Bilingual Education Office
Carolyn Minor, External Affairs Office
Mario Muniz, External Affairs Office
George Nemetz, Language Arts and Foreign Languages Unit

*Special consultants to the project.

In addition, the Department of Education commends the following members of the California Reading Association (CRA) for providing the annotations that appear in this publication:

James Macon, Educational Consultant (Past President, CRA); and Chairperson, Annotation Committee
Jeanne Ahern, Retired (Past CRA Board Member)
Diana Aldrich, Cupertino Union Elementary School District
Yvonne Ankele, Stockton City Unified School District
Jan Beekman, Ceres Unified School District
Ashley Bishop, California State University, Fullerton
Joan Blumenstein, Orange County Public Library, Costa Mesa
Anne Brietenberger, Walnut Valley Unified School District, Walnut
Julie Chan, Office of the Orange County Superintendent of Schools, Costa Mesa
Mildred Chatton, Professor Emeritus, San Jose State University
Sumie Childers, La Mesa-Spring Valley School District, La Mesa
Betty Chism, Office of the Modoc County Superintendent of Schools, Alturas
Barbara Cockerham, Riverside Unified School District (CRA Board Member)
Julia Candace Corliss, Mirman School for Gifted Children, Los Angeles
Marie Cottrell, Hacienda La Puente Unified School District, La Puente
Joan F. Curry,* San Diego State University (Vice-President, CRA)
Tom Cyr, Lucia Mar Unified School District, Arroyo Grande
Pat Dragon, South San Francisco Unified School District
Diane Flynn, Manteca Unified School District
Lorraine Godfrey,* Educational Consultant (Past CRA Board Member)
Rose Hehl, Anaheim Public Library
Mona Hellickson, Orange Unified School District
Rosemary Herndon, Turlock Joint Elementary School District
JoJo Hilliard, San Mateo County Librarian, San Mateo
Penny Hirschman,* Office of the San Bernardino County Superintendent of Schools (CRA Board Member)
Sachi Ishida, Lodi Unified School District
Marjorie Johnson, San Luis Coastal Unified School District, San Luis Obispo
Jack Jones, California Polytechnic State University, San Luis Obispo (Past President, CRA)
Joy Jones, San Luis Coastal Unified School District, San Luis Obispo
Karen Jones, Lucia Mar Unified School District, Arroyo Grande
Brady Kelso, San Diego City Unified School District
Elinore (Toni) Kenyon, Orange Unified School District
Jo Ann Keplinger, Lodi Unified School District
Kathie Kimmy, La Mesa-Spring Valley School District, La Mesa
Elizabeth Kreiger, San Luis Obispo Librarian
Sue Krumbein, Menlo Park City Elementary School District
Jan Lieberman,* University of Santa Clara
Margery Love, Orange Unified School District
Doris Lowry,* Retired, Stockton Unified School District
Joan Macon, Garden Grove Unified School District
Joan Mandato, Los Angeles Unified School District
Penny Markey, Los Angeles County Librarian
Vickie Meagher, Lucia Mar Unified School District, Arroyo Grande
Mercedes Monguia-Gifford, Orange County Public Library, Costa Mesa
Kathy Moore, Orange Unified School District
Lori Morgan,* Orange Unified School District (Vice-President Elect, CRA)
Faye Morrison, Palo Alto Unified School District
Linda Murphy, Office of the Humboldt County Superintendent of Schools, Eureka
Kathleen Naylor,* Hacienda La Puente Unified School District, La Puente (CRA Board Member)

*Area Coordinator, Annotation Committee

Ethel Neufeld, Stockton Unified School District
Jonnie Newcomer, Rialto Unified School District
Kay Niemeyer, Office of the San Diego County Superintendent of Schools
Linda Owen, Ceres Unified School District
Sharon Parravano, Modesto City Elementary School District
Carolyn Platt, Lucia Mar Unified School District, Arroyo Grande
Jane Prendergast, Duarte Unified School District
Lori Reuter, Orange County Public Library
Shirley Robertson, Retired Librarian
Deborah Schlanser, San Luis Obispo Librarian
Edna Sewill, San Jose Unified School District
Diane Shimoda, Orange Unified School District
Martha Silva, Lucia Mar Unified School District, Arroyo Grande
Richard Simpson, Lucia Mar Unified School District, Arroyo Grande
Barbara Skaggs, Coachella Valley Unified School District, Thermal
Sheri Sutterly, Turlock Joint Elementary School District
Barbara Swanson, Kern County Library System, Bakersfield
Pam Tarvin, Lucia Mar Unified School District, Arroyo Grande
Beverly Tavella, Hacienda La Puente Unified School District, La Puente
Suzanne Toaspern-Holm, Office of the Humboldt County Superintendent of Schools, Eureka
Judy Turner, Office of the Tehama County Superintendent of Schools, Red Bluff
Marge Ulrich, Evergreen Elementary School District, San Jose
Kathleen Underwood, Oak Grove Elemetary School District, San Jose
Jo Ann Valdez, Rialto Unified School District
Ellis Vance,* Clovis Unified School District (Past President, CRA)
Robin Velte, Office of the Siskiyou County Superintendent of Schools, Yreka
Sarah Villamil, Orange Unified School District
Kathy Villeneuve, Victor Valley Union High School District, Victorville
Maryellen Vogt,* University of California, Berkeley (Past CRA Board Member)
Becca Wachtmann,* California State Polytechnic University, San Luis Obispo, (Past President, CRA)
Linda Wallis, Riverside Unified School District
Kathy Weed, California State University, San Bernardino
Jean Wobbe, Tracy Elementary School District
Kathy Woods, Lompoc Unified School District
Steve Worth,* Redding Elementary School District (CRA Board Member)
Sandra Zevely, Office of the San Diego County Superintendent of Schools

Special appreciation is extended to the following individuals for their contributions:

Lynn Eisenhut, Coordinator of Children's Services, Orange County Public Library
Doris Lowry, School Librarian, Retired
Heath Lowry, Professor Emeritus, University of the Pacific, Stockton (Past President, CRA)
Donavan Merck, Former Manager, Language Arts and Foreign Languages Unit, California State Department of Education
Paula Pitluk, Librarian, Tetzlaff Junior High School, ABC Unified School District, Cerritos
Joyce Roth, District Librarian, ABC Unified School District, Cerritos

*Area Coordinator, Annotation Committee.

INTRODUCTION

primary goal for teaching literature is for children and young adults to discover the pleasure and the illumination that a fine piece of literature offers. Another significant goal is for pupils to become lifelong readers of literature. Through the reading of literature, pupils may experience vicariously the lives of others, different time periods, places, value systems, and the many cultures of the world.

This document contains recommended readings for pupils in kindergarten through grade eight. Local educators are encouraged to use these recommendations when reviewing their English language arts curriculum and when selecting literature to implement that curriculum.

Basic Intent of This Document

This list of readings is intended only as a guide for local-level policymakers, curriculum planners, teachers, and librarians; *it is not intended to be prescriptive in any way*. Local educators should encourage parents to become involved in the selection process of literature for the core program and for the independent reading program. Finally, this document is intended to encourage educators to review their literature programs and the accompanying instructional materials.

Development of the List

The development of the list involved many educators who used many reference resources as well as their own experience in classrooms at all levels. At the outset a list of some 2,000 titles of books that represent the spectrum of children's literature was established. The task of refining this list fell to educators: administrators, curriculum planners, classroom teachers, librarians, university-level educators, and members of statewide ethnic advisory committees. These educators suggested deletions of items that were deemed not suitable and suggested additions of titles that had not appeared earlier. This document, then, was developed by California educators for use by planners, teachers, and librarians in the elementary schools.

Local Decision-making Processes and Materials Selection Policies

This document is a resource that reflects the ideas of thoughtful educators from around the state. However, decisions about local programs and materials for those programs must be made at the local level. To make these local decisions, each school or school district should have a materials selection policy that guides the purchase of materials for instruction and for school and classroom libraries. This policy should include a provision for a materials selection committee that, at the minimum, includes in its membership: administrators, curriculum planners, librarians, classroom teachers, and community representatives.

Format of This Document

When selecting the format for this document, the developers were guided by one objective: to make the document easy to understand and to use. To accomplish this objective, the advisory committee decided to:

1. Divide the list into three sections that would cover all the entries. The sections are "Core and Extended Materials," "Recreational and Motivational Materials," and "Materials for Students in Grades Seven and Eight."
2. List the titles within these sections by traditional categories that are generally well-known by elementary teachers.
3. List each entry alphabetically by author or by title if it has no author.
4. Use a matrix to give helpful information that will assist local selectors of titles when searching for or selecting books.
5. Provide an index of authors and titles at the end of the document.

When teachers, librarians, and program planners use the lists, they will have a matrix to the right of each entry with special information to assist them. Many educators will not need to use the matrix, but for those who do, the columns have been designed accordingly:

1. Core and extended materials are designated by using the letters *C* and *E*.
2. The grade spans have been suggested by the committee members and are not prescriptive in any way. Local educators may opt to introduce certain works at different levels.
3. The literary contributions of specific ethnic or cultural groups are identified by one of the following symbols:

B	— Black	I	— American Indian
C	— Chinese	J	— Japanese
F	— Filipino	K	— Korean
H	— Hispanic	V	— Vietnamese

Finally, to give better information on the books about American Indians, the tribe, group, or band dealt with in the book is designated after each title.

Terms Used

In the lists that follow, titles are classified as core literature, extended literature, or recreational-motivational literature. This classification is used to assist local educators as they develop their programs and compile their own lists. The three types of literature are defined as follows:

Core literature. Core literature includes those selections that are to be *taught* in the classroom, are given close reading and intensive consideration, and are likely to be an important stimulus for writing and discussion. The core list should contain works of compelling, intellectual, social, or moral content. The core literature must be examples of excellent language use. District materials selection committees develop the basic list of core titles that teachers use in their classes.

Extended literature. Extended literature includes works that a teacher may assign to individual students or small groups of students to read for homework or individual reading to supplement classwork. Literature in the extended list also has emotional and aesthetic substance.

Recreational-motivational literature. Teachers and librarians should suggest recreational-motivational works to guide students when they are selecting individual, leisure-time reading materials from classroom, school, and community libraries. This type of literature may include works of special appeal to individual readers as well as works of universal appeal to all students.

Literature for All Students

The recommended readings listed in this document are for students in kindergarten through grade eight. Works of fiction, nonfiction, poetry, and drama have been chosen to accommodate a variety of tastes, abilities, and learning modalities. The selections include works about other cultures and works by authors that contribute to our common culture; works written or translated into foreign languages for children who read another language better than they do English; the classics, including modern-day classics; and just good reading books for children to enjoy.

Literature for Students in the Elementary Grades

This list of recommended readings is a resource that elementary school teachers and their curriculum planners may use to develop a literature program that has both scope and sequence. It is important that children at each grade level have experience with literature of a number of types and genres. They should be reading and hearing fiction and nonfiction, poetry and prose, and drama. Their experiences with fiction should include materials from the oral tradition, such as folklore and myth, modern fantasy, realistic adventure, and historical fiction.

The literature program is an essential part of the reading program and is as important as the developmental, basal reading materials. As students read and respond to literature regularly and systematically, thinking processes, critical reading skills, and the ability to interpret and explain what is written will improve as well. As children participate in imaginative writing activities, their interest in reading will be enhanced.

As the literature program is developed, curriculum planners must be careful to include materials from varied cultures. Because these materials contribute to understanding and mutual respect, they are as important for members of non-minority groups as well as for those in the minority groups. This list includes and identifies such literature.

If a program of literature is to succeed, parental cooperation is very important. The recreational reading will usually be done outside the school setting, and encouragement and interest in the students' homes will certainly reinforce what the school is saying about the importance and value of reading. Thus, when the program is being initiated, advisory groups of parents and other community members may help with the school-home communication.

The literature program is for all children. Those who cannot yet read English can read books in their first languages. While the primary emphasis in a literature program is on reading, important adjuncts to the curriculum are films, tapes, dramatic presentations, and above all, the teacher's systematic reading to the children. The most able readers as well as the least able readers benefit from hearing good literature read aloud.

The love of reading is one of the most important gifts that teachers and parents may give to children. Literature will provide experiences that are ordinarily inaccessible to students, broaden their knowledge of the world and its people, and improve reading skills, such as decoding and comprehension. Literature is one of the basics and should be taught in all curricular areas.

CORE AND EXTENDED MATERIALS

This section contains lists of core and extended materials. It is designed to suggest works to district materials selection committees and teachers. For easier use, the entries are divided by categories; a matrix is provided to give users some information about the listed works.

The categories are Picture Books, Folklore, Modern Fantasy and Science Fiction, Poetry, Contemporary Realistic Fiction, Historical Fiction, Nonfiction—Information, Nonfiction—Biography, Plays, and Books in Languages Other Than English.

The columns of the matrix indicate the type of entry, i.e., core (C) or extended (E) (see definitions in the introduction to the document), and the grade span where the work should be introduced. When the entry concerns literary contributions of specific ethnic or cultural groups, the ethnic or cultural group is indicated (see the introduction for a listing of the groups).

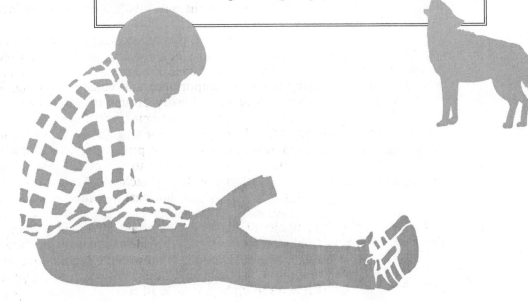

PICTURE BOOKS

Picture books are a literary genre in and of themselves. These books are an artistry of both word and illustration, the masterful interplay of text and image. In selecting the finest in available picture books, the person making the selections should keep these three standards in mind: the intrinsic artistic quality of the illustrations themselves, the literary merit of the text, and the interrelationship of words and pictures. The illustrations ought to extend and enhance the text and, frequently, tell parts of the story not explicitly stated in the text.

Because there are many ways of sharing picture books, they are a delight to use with the primary-level child. Reading aloud, picture book storytelling, the individual reading, or simply "reading" from the pictures are all possibilities for the beginning reader. Students can create the entire text by using wordless picture books as a focus; they can hear a story and then retell it by using the picture book as a sequencing aid.

Older students can appreciate comparing many illustrated books by the same artist, such as Trina S. Hyman, or different artists' illustrations for the same story, such as "Hansel and Gretel," for example.

	Type of entry	Grade level	Culture
Anno, Mitsumasa. *Anno's Counting Book.* Crowell, 1977. Young readers find a stimulating adventure of imagination by entering the world of counting and numbers. They can be led to see and understand the real meaning of numbers, groups, and sets.	C	K–2	
Bang, Molly G. *Ten, Nine, Eight.* Greenwillow, 1983; Penguin, 1985. Reminiscent of "One, two, buckle my shoe," this rhythmic verse goes in reverse order, ten to one, to describe washing up, getting nightclothes on, good-night cuddles, and so forth.	E	K–1	B
Bate, Lucy. *Little Rabbit's Loose Tooth.* Crown, 1975. Little Rabbit solves the problem of what to do with her loose tooth when it comes out in a dish of chocolate ice cream	E	K–2	
Bemmelmans, Ludwig. *Madeline.* Viking, 1939; Penguin, 1977. Madeline lives with 11 other small girls in a Paris home. After her appendectomy, her friends examine her scar and the toys and gifts she received. They decide they want an appendectomy, too.	E	K–3	
Burton, Virginia L. *The Little House.* Houghton, 1942, 1978. A small country house is being encroached on by the growing city. The house is saved when a couple moves her out of the city and back to the country where she is cared for once again.	C	K–2	

	Type of entry	Grade level	Culture

Carle, Eric. *One, Two, Three, to the Zoo.* World, 1968. — C, K–2
With illustrations instead of text, this book provides an interesting approach to numbers and sets as animals ride to their new zoo home.

Carle, Eric. *The Very Busy Spider.* Putnam, 1984. — E, K–2
A spider perseveres to build a web despite distracting invitations by the barnyard animals.

Carle, Eric. *The Very Hungry Caterpillar.* Putnam, 1981. — C, K–2
A hungry caterpillar eats through ten things as the reader turns pages in which there are holes.

Clifton, Lucille. *Everett Anderson's Nine Month Long.* Holt, 1978. — E, K–2, B
A small boy and his family anticipate the birth of a new member to the household.

Cohen, Miriam. *Starring First Grade.* Greenwillow, 1985. — E, K–1
Jim and his classmates from *Will I Have a Friend?* plan a production of the "Three Billy Goats Gruff" for the school assembly.

Cooney, Barbara. *Miss Rumphius.* Viking, 1982. — C, K–3
Great-Aunt Alice Rumphius was once a little girl who loved the sea, longed to visit faraway places, and wished to do something to make the world more beautiful.

Crews, Donald. *Freight Train.* Greenwillow, 1978. — C, K–1
Brief text and illustrations trace the journey of a colorful train as it goes through tunnels, by cities, and over trestles.

De Regniers, Beatrice S. *May I Bring a Friend?* Atheneum, 1964. — C, K–2
A repetitive, rhyming text and lively illustrations describe a small boy's receiving an invitation to tea from the king and queen, with any or all of his four-legged friends.

Duvoisin, Roger. *Petunia.* Knopf, 1950. — E, K–2
This picture book with a moral recounts the adventures of Petunia the goose. Petunia finds a book and, believing mere possession of it will make her wise, sets off on a series of misadventures that cause her barnyard friends a lot of trouble.

Feelings, Muriel. *Jambo Means Hello: Swahili Alphabet Book.* Dial Books, 1974. — E, 3–6, B
According to the author, the book is intended to introduce the reader to Swahili words. Black-and-white paintings accent this A-B-C dictionary of Swahili terms and definitions.

Feelings, Muriel. *Moja Means One: Swahili Counting Book.* Illustrated by Tom Feelings. Dial Books, 1971. — C, 2–5, B
Focusing on the Swahili language of Central Africa, the author and her illustrator husband present the numbers one through ten in pictures with descriptive scenes.

	Type of entry	Grade level	Culture

Flack, Marjorie. *Ask Mister Bear.* Macmillan, 1932, 1958, 1960. — E, K-1

This picture book is about a little boy who wonders what to give his mother for her birthday. His friend, Mister Bear, tells him what the best present of all would be.

Freeman, Don. *Corduroy.* Viking, 1968; Puffin, 1976. — C, K-2

This story is about the search of a teddy bear through a department store for a friend. His quest ends when a little girl buys him with her piggy-bank savings.

Gackenbach, Dick. *Harry and the Terrible Whatzit.* Seabury Press, 1977. — C, K-2

Harry's mother goes to the cellar and does not return right away. He goes down to search for her and confronts the terrible two-headed whatzit.

Gag, Wanda. *The ABC Bunny.* Coward, 1933. — E, K-1

A small bunny learns his letters and a lot more in this classic black-and-white alphabet book. (A piano arrangement is included.)

Gag, Wanda. *Millions of Cats.* Coward, 1928. — E, K-2

This story is about an old man who set out to get his lonely wife a cat and almost got hundreds of cats, millions and billions of cats.

Hoban, Russell. *Bread and Jam for Frances.* Illustrated by Lillian Hoban. Harper, 1964. — C, K-3

Frances's wise mother cures her daughter from being a food faddist. At the end of the story, a wonderful lunchbox packed with lobster salad, black olives, and cherries is provided.

Hoban, Tana. *A, B, See!* Greenwillow, 1982. — E, K-1

A collection is presented of photographs of objects whose names begin with a particular letter of the alphabet.

Hoban, Tana. *A Children's Zoo.* Greenwillow, 1985. — C, 1-3

Answers to queries about animals appear, such as: Where do they come from? Where do they live? What do they eat? This colorful picture book of birds and mammals features concept words (for example, black, white, and fuzzy) which characterize each animal.

Hoban, Tana. *Over, Under and Through and Other Spatial Concepts.* Macmillan, 1973. — E, K-3

In brief text and photographs, the author depicts several spatial concepts: over, under, through, on, in, around, across, between, beside, below, against, and behind.

Hutchins, Pat. *Changes, Changes.* Macmillan, 1971. — E, 2-5

Bright-colored building blocks and wooden dolls create their own adventures and solve their own problems as they progress from house to fire engine, to barge, to truck, to locomotive, and back home.

	Type of entry	Grade level	Culture

Hutchins, Pat. *Rosie's Walk.* Macmillan, 1968.   **C**   **K–6**

Rosie the hen goes for a walk around the farm and gets home in time for dinner, completely unaware that a fox has been on her heels every step of the way. The fox, however, is foiled at every turn by the unwitting hen.

Kantrowitz, Mildred. *Maxie.* Parents Magazine Press, 1970.   **C**   **2–4**

This story is about a woman who feels no one needs her. When she does not follow her daily routines, her neighbors become concerned and visit her apartment. Maxie realizes that she is important to others.

Keats, Ezra J. *Snowy Day.* Viking, 1962.   **C**   **K–1**   **B**

A small boy's delight and enjoyment of snow in the city is shown in vibrant illustrations.

Kraus, Robert. *Leo the Late Bloomer.* Illustrated by José Aruego and Ariane Aruego. Crowell, 1971.   **E**   **2–4**

Distressed by his inability to read, write, talk, and so forth, young Leo feels even worse when his father expresses concern about his son's backwardness. His mother reassures Leo's father with her statement, "Leo is just a late bloomer." Her words have proved comforting to many children who have identified with the young tiger.

Krauss, Ruth. *The Carrot Seed.* Illustrated by Crockett Johnson. Harper and Row, 1945.   **C**   **K–2**

Simple text and pictures show how the faith of a small boy who planted a carrot seed was rewarded.

MacDonald, Golden (Margaret Wise Brown). *The Little Island.* Illustrated by Leonard Weisgard. Doubleday, 1946.   **E**   **1–4**

A poetic text with pictures describes changes that occur on a small island as seasons come and go, as day changes to night, and as a storm approaches.

Marshall, James E. *George and Martha.* Houghton, 1974.   **C**   **1–4**

This story relates several episodes in the friendship of two hippopotamuses.

Martin, Bill, Jr. *Brown Bear, Brown Bear, What Do You See?* Holt, 1983.   **C**   **K–2**

A story told in rhyme responds to the question, What do you see? Each answer leads to further questions regarding more colors and animals.

McCloskey, Robert. *Blueberries for Sal.* Viking, 1948.   **E**   **K–3**

The author-artist tells what happens on a summer day in Maine when a little girl and a bear cub wander away from their blueberry-picking mothers, and each mistakes the other's mother for its own.

McCloskey, Robert. *Make Way for Ducklings.* Viking, 1941.   **C**   **K–6**

This Caldecott Medal award winner is a picturesque and amusing story of a family of baby ducklings born on the Charles River near Boston. They are assisted by a friendly policeman when they cross through Boston traffic to the pond in the public gardens.

	Type of entry	Grade level	Culture

Musgrove, Margaret. *Ashanti to Zulu: African Traditions.* Illustrated by Leo Dillon and Diane Dillon. Dial Books, 1976.

> This Caldecott Medal award winner with full-page illustrations and brief texts describes African tribes and their customs. The richly colored illustrations show the people in typical dress and their land, animals, and homes.

C · 3–6 · B

A Peaceable Kingdom: The Shaker Abecedarius. Illustrated by Alice Provensen and Martin Provensen. Viking, 1978.

> Shaker designs and colors decorate this abecedarius, "a 26-line verse that has a successive letter of the alphabet at the beginning of each line." Illustrations also provide insight into the simple Shaker culture.

E · 3–6

Politi, Leo. *The Nicest Gift.* Scribner, 1973.

> Carlitos lives in the Mexican-dominated barrio of East Los Angeles, enjoying its picturesque life with his dog Blanco, until Blanco gets lost. Carlitos is brokenhearted until he and his dog are reunited at a Christmas mass.

E · K–8 · H

Potter, Beatrix. *The Tale of Peter Rabbit.* Warne, 1903.

> This story is about Peter Rabbit, who disobeys his mother and goes into Mr. McGregor's garden.

C · K–2

Rosario, Idalia. *Idalia's Project ABC—Proyecto ABC: An Urban Alphabet Book in English and Spanish.* Holt, 1981.

> A letter on each page with a sentence in English and Spanish introduces the alphabet in a brief description of city life.

C · K–2 · H

Schweitzer, Byrd Baylor. *Amigo.* Macmillan, 1963.

> This rhyming story is about a Mexican boy living in desert country who wants a dog. The family does not have enough food for a real one, so Francisco tries to tame a prairie dog.

E · 3–5 · H

Scott, Ann Herbert. *Sam.* McGraw-Hill, 1967.

> This read-aloud book is about an episode in Sam's life. Sam's mother, father, and older brother and sister continually tell him, "Don't touch! Go away!" Then they find a job that is just right for Sam.

E · K–3 · B

Slobodkina, Esphyr. *Caps for Sale.* Harper Junior Books, 1947.

> This read-aloud book is about a cap peddler who takes a nap under a tree, only to discover when he wakes up that his caps are all gone. When he looks up at the tree, he sees countless monkeys, each wearing a cap and grinning with glee.

C · K–2

Turkle, Brinton. *Deep in the Forest.* Dutton, 1976.

> This book has no text, except for the names on the bowls. The story is a reverse of "Goldilocks and the Three Bears." An inquisitive bear cub discovers a log cabin and samples food, chairs, and beds. The havoc he creates is discovered by a little girl and her parents when they return from a walk.

C · K–4

	Type of entry	Grade level	Culture

Udry, Janice M. *What Mary Jo Shared.* Whitman, 1966.

    Whenever Mary Jo selected something to "show and tell," her classmates had already chosen it. Finally, she brings her father to share his experiences with her class.

Type of entry: E   *Grade level:* K–1   *Culture:* B

Viorst, Judith. *Alexander and the Terrible, Horrible, No Good, Very Bad Day.* Illustrated by Ray Cruz. Atheneum, 1972.

    The plight of a boy who had a bad day is described. The moment he gets out of bed, he discovers he has gum stuck to his hair. When he returns to bed, he has to wear his hated railroad train pajamas. Even the cat decides to sleep with his brother instead of with him. His mother consoles him by saying, "Some days are like that."

Type of entry: C   *Grade level:* 1–6

Viorst, Judith. *The Tenth Good Thing About Barney.* Atheneum, 1971.

    A little boy saddened by the death of his cat thinks of nine good things about Barney to say at his funeral. Later his father helps him discover a tenth good thing.

Type of entry: E   *Grade level:* K–3

Waber, Bernard. *Ira Sleeps Over.* Houghton, 1972.

    A small boy's joy in being asked to spend the night with a friend who lives next door knows no bounds until his sister raises the question of whether or not he should take his teddy bear.

Type of entry: C   *Grade level:* 1–3

Ward, Lynd. *The Biggest Bear.* Houghton, 1972.

    Johnny goes hunting and brings home a cuddly bear cub. Its size and appetite grow to immense proportions, causing Johnny's family and neighbors to become worried.

Type of entry: C   *Grade level:* K–3

Wildsmith, Brian. *Brian Wildsmith's ABC.* Watts, 1962.

    This alphabet book illustrates animals and objects, identifying each on a facing page in capital and lowercase letters. The first letter is set off with special emphasis.

Type of entry: E   *Grade level:* K–1

Zion, Gene. *Harry, the Dirty Dog.* Harper Junior Books, 1956.

    A white dog with black spots hates baths and runs away. He returns in such a sad condition that even the family members do not recognize him.

Type of entry: E   *Grade level:* K–3

Zolotow, Charlotte. *William's Doll.* Harper Junior Books, 1972.

    When little William asks for a doll, his father tries to interest him in boys' playthings such as a basketball and a train. His grandmother buys him the doll, explaining his need to have it to love and care for so that he can practice being a father.

Type of entry: E   *Grade level:* K–2

FOLKLORE

Folklore exerts its appeal down through the ages and in widely separated cultures because it deals with the deepest human feelings and experiences. By reading the stories, children can enjoy the puzzles of good and evil, fear and courage, wisdom and folly, fortune and misfortune, cruelty and kindness. The tales help readers and listeners to explain the world and to bridge its confusing dimensions.

	Type of entry	Grade level	Culture
Aardema, Verna. ***Bringing the Rain to Kapiti Plain.*** Dial Books, 1981. This African rhyming folktale tells how Ki-pat, the herdsman, works out a clever method to save the plain from a long drought.	C	1–4	B
Aardema, Verna. ***Why Mosquitoes Buzz in People's Ears: A West African Tale.*** Illustrated by Leo Dillon and Diane Dillon. Dial Books, 1975. This interesting folktale begins with a mosquito teasing an iguana. The panic is contagious. Through use of the "House That Jack Built" rhyme, all of the trouble is finally traced right back to the mosquito.	C	1–4	B
Aesop. ***Aesop's Fables.*** Illustrated by Heidi Holder. Viking, 1981. This collection of nine fables is retold with Rackman-style illustrations, which are done in pen and ink and finished in watercolor.	C	2–6	
Anansi the Spider: A Tale from the Ashanti. Retold and illustrated by Gerald McDermott. Holt, 1972. In this story a spider that is saved from a terrible fate by his six sons is unable to decide which of them to reward. The solution to his predicament is also an explanation for how the moon was put into the sky.	E	3–6	B
Asbjornsen, Peter Christian, and Jorgen E. Moe. ***East of the Sun and West of the Moon and Other Tales.*** Illustrated by Mercer Mayer. Four Winds Press, 1980. In this Norwegian folktale, the Moon, Father Forest, Great Fish of the Sea, and North Wind help a maiden rescue her true love from a troll princess in a faraway kingdom.	C	4–6	
Baker, Olaf. ***Where the Buffaloes Begin.*** Frederick Warne, 1981. In this tale Little Wolf, a courageous boy, longs to find the lake where the buffaloes begin. His adventure comes to an end with a wild and unforgettable ride through the night to save his people.	E	5–8	

	Type of entry	Grade level	Culture
Baylor, Byrd. *And It Is Still That Way.* Scribner, 1976. In this collection of legends told by Arizona Indian children, the traditional Indian tales have been included. The author includes information about the tradition of storytelling among the Indians.	E	2-4	
Beauty and the Beast. Retold by Marianna Mayer. Four Winds Press, 1978. Through her great capacity to love, a kind and beautiful maid releases a handsome prince from the spell that has made him an ugly beast.	C	3-6	
Blair, Walter. *Tall Tale America.* Illustrated by Glen Rounds. Coward, 1944. This legendary history of our humorous heroes includes Captain Stormalong, Jonathan Slick, Mike Fink, Febold Feboldson, Paul Bunyan, Davy Crockett, Pecos Bill, John Henry, and numerous others.	C	4-6	
Briggs, Raymond. *Jim and the Beanstalk.* Coward, 1970; Putnam, 1980. Jim climbs up the beanstalk and encounters the giant from whom his father, Jack, stole the golden hen. The giant is old, bald, toothless, and very nearsighted. Jim gains the giant's confidence and helps him feel and look young again.	E	3-5	
Brown, Marcia. *Once a Mouse.* Scribner, 1961. Woodcuts provide memorable illustrations for a fable from India that retells what happens when a hermit changes a frightened mouse first into a cat, then a dog, and finally a tiger.	C	2-4	
Brown, Marcia. *Stone Soup.* Scribner, 1947. When hungry soldiers get a chilly reception in a village, they use a clever trick to get a meal.	C	1-4	
Brown, Marcia, and Charles Perrault. *Cinderella.* Illustrated by Marcia Brown. Scribner, 1954. In this version, which is a translation from the French of Charles Perrault, Marcia Brown has freely translated the original story of Cinderella. This translation is an excellent choice to use for reading aloud or storytelling.	C	1-4	
Bryan, Ashley. *Beat the Story-Drum, Pum-Pum.* Atheneum, 1980. The five Nigerian folktales are told in rhythmic language and with bold woodcuts printed in ochre, red, and black.	C	5-6	B
Carpenter, Frances. *Tales of a Korean Grandmother.* Doubleday, 1947; Tuttle, 1972. Thirty-two rich Korean folktales are contrasted with the life—past and present—of the Kim family. Each tale has a mixture of fact, fancy, and genuine folklore.	C	K-4	K

	Type of entry	Grade level	Culture

Chase, Richard. *The Jack Tales.* Riverside, 1943.

These stories of American folklore have been handed down from generation to generation in the oral tradition. In these tales, a seemingly nonheroic person overcomes severe obstacles to outwit adversaries.

Type of entry: C *Grade level:* 4–6

Chicken Little. Retold and illustrated by Steven Kellogg. William Morrow, 1985.

In this modern version Chicken Little and the feathered friends, alarmed that the sky seems to be falling, are easy prey to hungry Foxy Loxy when he poses as a police officer in hopes of tricking them into his "poulice" truck.

Type of entry: C *Grade level:* 1–3

Ching, Annie. *Birthday Party (and Other Tales).* Asian American Bilingual Center, Berkeley, 1979.

A five-year-old Filipino girl is disappointed, because she is unable to get a better birthday gift from her father.

Type of entry: E *Grade level:* K–6 *Culture:* C

Coburn, Jewell R. *Encircled Kingdom: Legends and Folktales of Laos.* Burn-Hart, 1979.

These are stories of Laotian life and culture.

Type of entry: E *Grade level:* 4–6

The Cow-Tail Switch and Other West African Stories. Retold by Harold Courlander and George Herzog. Putnam, 1982.

This collection of humorous West African folktales reflects the spirit of the original tellers.

Type of entry: E *Grade level:* 5–6 *Culture:* B

D'Aulaire, Ingri, and Edgar P. D'Aulaire. *D'Aulaires' Book of Greek Myths.* Doubleday, 1962.

Young readers will find this book appealing. The Greek myths about the gods, the titans, and the heroes are told in a simple narrative style. The volume is large and beautifully illustrated.

Type of entry: C *Grade level:* 4–6

D'Aulaire, Ingri, and Edgar P. D'Aulaire. *Norse Gods and Giants.* Doubleday, 1967.

The authors retell the dramatic, exciting, and often humorous tales of Norse mythology for young children.

Type of entry: E *Grade level:* 3–6

Dayrell, Elphinstone. *Why the Sun and Moon Live in the Sky.* Houghton, 1968.

In this old African folktale, the storyteller explains how the Sun, the Moon, and the Water came to be where they are.

Type of entry: C *Grade level:* 3–5 *Culture:* B

DePaola, Tomie. *Strega Nona.* Prentice-Hall, 1975.

In this hilarious, exaggerated tale, Big Anthony uses the magic words to start spaghetti making; but he does not know how to turn the magic off.

Type of entry: C *Grade level:* 1–4

Duong, Van Quyen, and Jewell Reinhart Coburn. *Beyond the East Wind: Legends and Folktales of Vietnam.* Burn-Hart, 1976.

Ten tales explain such things as the origin of Vietnam, the meaning behind Vietnamese wedding ceremony symbols and New Year's refreshments, and the legend of the monsoon rains. A brief history of the country, with comments and explanations, is included.

Type of entry: E *Grade level:* 4–8 *Culture:* V

	Type of entry	Grade level	Culture

Fleischman, Sid. *Humbug Mountain*. Little, 1978.

    Humorous, suspenseful, and original, this book tells the exciting adventures of the Flint family as they battle outlaws, ghosts, creditors, and others on the banks of the Missouri River in the late 1800s.

C   4–6

Gag, Wanda. *Tales from Grimm*. Coward, 1936.

    Translations of 16 tales from Grimm are true to the original spirit of the stories.

C   4–6

Galdone, Paul. *Jack and the Beanstalk*. Clarion, 1982.

    This is the familiar tale of Jack and his adventures to regain his possessions from the giant. Colorful, humorous illustrations appear.

C   1–4

Galdone, Paul. *The Little Red Hen*. Clarion, 1973.

    A little hen works for her lazy housemates in this reworking of the old tale. Animated characterizations illustrated in warm, rustic colors appear.

E   K–2

Galdone, Paul. *The Three Bears*. Scholastic, 1973.

    The illustrations for this familiar story of the three bears and their visitor, Goldilocks, are colorful and humorous.

C   K–2

Galdone, Paul. *The Three Billy Goats Gruff*. Clarion, 1981.

    The author's special feeling for animals and nature results in a fresh interpretation of this classic children's tale.

C   1–3

Gates, Doris. *Lord of the Sky: Zeus*. Viking, 1972.

    In the first of a series, the author has retold simply and directly myths in which Zeus plays a central part.

C   6

Goble, Paul. *Buffalo Woman*. Bradbury, 1984.

    This legend from the Plains Indians about a buffalo that turns into a beautiful girl tells of the kinship between man and animal.

E   3–6   I

Goble, Paul. *The Girl Who Loved Wild Horses* (Plains). Bradbury, 1978.

    With simple words and brilliant paintings, the author tells the story of an American Indian girl and her love of horses.

C   4–8   I

Granfa' Grig Had a Pig and Other Rhymes Without Reason from Mother Goose. Composed and illustrated by Wallace Tripp. Little, 1976.

    This book contains a collection of animal people with keenly expressive faces. Most double-page spreads show several rhymes with an accompanying illustration.

C   K–6

Griego, Margot C., and others. *Tortillitas para mamá: And Other Spanish Nursery Rhymes*. Holt, 1987.

    Children of all ages and adults, too, will treasure this collection of Latin-American nursery rhymes.

C   K–3   H

	Type of entry	Grade level	Culture

Grimm, Jacob, and Wilhelm Grimm. *The Bremen Town Musicians.* Doubleday, 1980. — C — 1–3

This famous folktale is about four animals that, in an attempt to become musicians, frighten away some robbers.

Grimm, Jacob, and Wilhelm Grimm. *The Devil with the Three Golden Hairs.* Knopf, 1983. — E — 3–5

To keep his princess bride, a young man must collect three golden hairs from the devil's head.

Grimm, Jacob, and Wilhelm Grimm. *Little Red Riding Hood.* Retold and illustrated by Trina S. Hyman. Holiday House, 1983. — C — 2–5

A favorite tale is retold of a little girl and her encounter with a wolf on the way to her grandmother's house.

Grimm, Jacob, and Wilhelm Grimm. *Rapunzel.* Retold by Barbara Rogasky and illustrated by Trina S. Hyman. Holiday House, 1982. — E — 2–5

The famous tale of the captive princess and her fabulous long hair is retold. The colorful illustrations make this edition a classic.

Grimm, Jacob, and Wilhelm Grimm. *The Shoemaker and the Elves.* Illustrated by Adrienne Adams. Scribner, 1982. — E — 1–3

This favorite German tale is about an honest but poor shoemaker who is visited by elves at night. In return for the elves' helpfulness, the shoemaker and his wife devise a perfect gift.

Grimm, Jacob, and Wilhelm Grimm. *Snow-White and the Seven Dwarfs.* Illustrated by Nancy Ekholm Burkert. Farrar, 1972. — C — 3–6

This famous story tells of seven caring dwarfs and their lovely charge, Snow White.

Haley, Gail E. *A Story, a Story.* Atheneum, 1970. — C — 1–4 — B

How African "spider stories" began is traced back to the time when Anansi, the Spider Man, made a bargain with the Sky God.

Hastings, Selina. *Sir Gawain and the Green Knight.* Lothrop, 1981. — E — 5–6

The Green Knight challenges young Gawain to strike off his head on the condition that one year later the Green Knight can do the same to him.

Hien, Nguyen Thai Duc. *Doi song moi/Tren dat moi: A New Life in a New Land.* National Assessment and Dissemination Center, 1980. — C — 4–8 — V

This fourth-grade reader for Vietnamese students tells of adjusting to a new life in America.

Hodges, Margaret. *The Wave.* Houghton, 1964. — C — 1–4 — J

A wise old Japanese farmer burns his rice fields to warn the people in the village of an approaching tidal wave.

	Type of entry	Grade level	Culture

Hogrogian, Nonny. *One Fine Day.* Macmillan, 1971.

	C	1–4	

A greedy fox sets off a chain of events when he drinks the milk from the pail of an old woman, who then cuts off his tail.

Jaquith, Priscilla. *Bo Rabbit Smart for True: Folktales from the Gullah.* Philomel, 1981.

	C	4–6	B

In these animal tales the common theme is the deflating of the smug and self-satisfied.

Jataka Tales. Edited by Nancy DeRoin and illustrated by Ellen Lanyon. Houghton, 1975.

	E	3–6	

Modern-day problems, such as responsibility, honesty, respect for the old, and preservation of the ecological order, have been included in this retelling of some of the tales originally told by Buddha.

Keats, Ezra Jack. *John Henry: An American Legend.* Pantheon, 1965.

	C	2–5	B

John Henry, the railroad hero, was born with and died with a hammer in his hand.

Kipling, Rudyard. *The Elephant's Child.* Harcourt, 1983.

	E	4–6	

On the banks of the "great green, greasy Limpopo River," a young elephant gains knowledge and a trunk from his teacher, the crocodile.

Lang, Andrew. *Aladdin and the Wonderful Lamp.* Viking, 1981.

	E	4–6	

Aladdin, with the aid of a genie from a magic lamp, fights an evil magician and wins the hand of a beautiful princess.

Lester, Julius. *The Knee-High Man and Other Tales.* Dial Books, 1972.

	E	4–6	B

These six delightfully funny stories deal with animals and their problems; one explains nature, and the last two are concerned with man's stupidity and insatiable desires.

Lobel, Arnold. *Gregory Griggs and Other Nursery Rhyme People.* Greenwillow, 1978.

	E	2–6	

This collection of nursery rhymes is about humorous personalities and adventures of lesser known but unique individuals.

London Bridge Is Falling Down. Illustrated by Peter Spier. Doubleday, 1967.

	E	K–3	

The history of London Bridge is presented through detailed illustrations along with the words of the well-known nursery rhyme.

Louie, Ai-Lang. *Yeh Shen: A Cinderella Story from China.* Illustrated by Edward Young. Philomel, 1982.

	C	3–6	C

A young Chinese girl overcomes the wickedness of her stepsister and stepmother to become the bride of a prince.

Luenn, Nancy. *The Dragon Kite.* Harcourt, 1983.

	C	3–6	J

An unusual thief, Ishikawa, attempts to learn the skills of a kite-maker in order to steal the two golden dolphins that adorn the roof of Nagoya Castle.

	Type of entry	Grade level	Culture

McDermott, Gerald. *Arrow to the Sun: A Pueblo Indian Tale.* Viking, 1974.

A young boy journeys to the heavens to find his father, the Lord of the Sun.

E | 3–5 | I

The Merry Adventures of Robin Hood. Edited by Howard Pyle. Scribner, 1946.

In this well-known tale, Robin Hood and his followers have many adventures.

E | 6–8

Mosel, Arlene. *The Funny Little Woman.* Illustrated by Blair Lent. Dutton, 1972.

A giggly little lady from medieval Japan chases a rolling rice dumpling into a cavern, where she is captured by a fearsome *oni* who needs a good cook.

E | 2–5 | J

North American Legends. Edited by Virginia Haviland. Philomel, 1979.

In this selection are stories told by American Indians, Eskimos, and black Americans; tales brought by European immigrants; tall tales; and humorous stories from Appalachia.

C | 3–6 | I

Paul Bunyan. Retold by Steven Kellogg. Morrow, 1984.

This legendary character of Maine, Paul Bunyan, weighed 156 pounds at birth. Even as a young lad, he wrestled grizzly bears. With Babe, the super ox, he dug the Great Lakes and the Saint Lawrence River as he led a band of lumbermen westward.

C | 3–5

Roland, Donna. *Grandfather's Stories—Cambodia* and *More of Grandfather's Stories.* Open My World Publishing (P.O. Box 15011, San Diego, CA 92115).

The ten books in this series contain stories from Cambodia, Germany, Mexico, the Philippines, and Vietnam.

C | K–3

Rounds, Glen. *Ol' Paul: The Mighty Logger.* Holiday House, 1976.

This tall tale, republished in a fortieth anniversary edition, is illustrated by the author in a larger format, with clearer type, wider margins, and zany new pen-and-ink sketches. The exploits of the American folk hero Paul Bunyan and his super ox, Babe, can be read aloud.

E | 4–6

Saint George and the Dragon: A Golden Legend. Adapted by Margaret Hodges and illustrated by Trina S. Hyman. Little, 1984.

Trina Hyman's illustrations are richly colored, detailed, and dramatic in this retelling of this legend from Edmund Spenser's *Faerie Queene.* George, the Red Cross knight, slays the dreadful dragon that has been terrorizing the countryside for years and brings peace to the land.

E | 4–6

Shulevitz, Uri. *The Treasure.* Farrar, 1978.

Sometimes one must travel far to discover what is near. This eastern European aphorism is integrated in the present folktale. In this story an old man dreams thrice that a treasure is buried under a bridge in a far-off city. However, he finds the treasure buried in his own home.

E | 4–5

	Type of entry	Grade level	Culture

Singer, Isaac B. ***Zlateh the Goat and Other Stories.*** Harper, 1966.

The seven Jewish folklores of Poland are transformed with poetic power by the author and illustrator. The essence of human nature is exuberantly imparted in the stories.

(Type of entry: E, Grade level: 6–8)

The Sleeping Beauty by the Brothers Grimm. Illustrated by Trina S. Hyman. Little, 1976.

This is one of the great fairy tales that one generation repeats to another. The reader rejoices at love's power to triumph over the dark powers of revenge.

(Type of entry: C, Grade level: 2–4)

Steptoe, John. ***The Story of Jumping Mouse, a Native American Legend.*** Lothrop, 1984.

By keeping hope alive within himself, a mouse is successful in his quest for the far-off land.

(Type of entry: C, Grade level: 3–6, Culture: I)

Stoutenburg, Adrien. ***American Tall Tales.*** Viking, 1968.

Bears of incredible size and wit; talented rattlesnakes; fur-bearing trout; water-toting, humpbacked desert fish; and spirited horse mackerel are among the curious creatures that appear in this collection of fantastic American fauna. Descriptions of these entertaining animals were drawn from old newspapers, periodicals, and out-of-print books.

(Type of entry: E, Grade level: 4–7)

Suyeoka, George. ***Momotaro: Peach Boy.*** Island Heritage, 1972.

An extraordinary Japanese boy is determined to rid his village of the ogres who have terrorized the people for years.

(Type of entry: E, Grade level: K–2, Culture: J)

Two Brothers and Their Magic Gourds. Edited by Edward B. Adams. Tuttle, 1981.

This selection is part of the *Korean Folk Stories for Children* series.

(Type of entry: C, Grade level: 3–8, Culture: K)

Uchida, Yoshiko. ***The Magic Listening Cap: More Folktales from Japan.*** Harcourt, 1955.

Fourteen Japanese folktales are retold charmingly and humorously to give them wide appeal. These tales are appropriate for reading aloud or for storytelling.

(Type of entry: E, Grade level: 1–4, Culture: J)

Wolkstein, Diane. ***The Banza.*** Dial Books, 1984.

The length and clarity of the story make it an excellent selection for reading aloud. This is a tale of the small outwitting the large. Through the use of a banza, a musical stringed instrument, the goat is kept alive.

(Type of entry: C, Grade level: K–3, Culture: B)

Wyndham, Robert. ***Chinese Mother Goose Rhymes.*** Illustrated by Edward Young. Philomel, 1982.

This book, which has a vertical format, contains a collection of Chinese rhymes, riddles, and games, which have been retold to children for hundreds of years. The illustrations are in calligraphy.

(Type of entry: C, Grade level: K–3, Culture: C)

	Type of entry	Grade level	Culture

Yagawa, Sumiko. *The Crane Wife.* Translated by Katherine Paterson and illustrated by Suekichi Akaba. Morrow, 1981. — C, 4–6, J

Soon after the farmer tends to a crane, he acquires a beautiful wife who is an excellent weaver. The farmer is admonished never to watch while his wife is weaving. Impelled by greed and bad advice, he breaks his promise and the crane wife returns to her own people, never to be seen again.

Yashima, Taro. *Umbrella.* Viking, 1958. — C, K–3, J

A little Japanese girl living in New York City is given an umbrella and a pair of red rubber boots on her third birthday. Day after day, eagerly and impatiently, Momo waits for rain. When rain finally falls, beautiful colored pictures capture the child's joy and excitement.

Zemach, Harve. *Duffy and the Devil.* Illustrated by Margot Zemach. Farrar, 1976. — E, 3–5

In this humorous Cornish variation of the legend of Rumpelstiltskin, pastel coloring illustrates the story. The legend of Rumpelstiltskin has never seemed as funny as it does in this version by the author-artist team.

Zemach, Margot. *It Could Always Be Worse.* Farrar, 1976. — E, 1–4

The author-illustrator retells a Yiddish folktale of the simple villager whose house was so crowded and noisy that he went to the rabbi for help. The rabbi told the frantic man to bring his livestock into the house and to remove them when the commotion became unbearable.

THE SINGLE MOST IMPORTANT ACTIVITY FOR BUILDING THE KNOWLEDGE REQUIRED FOR EVENTUAL SUCCESS IN READING IS READING ALOUD TO CHILDREN.

MODERN FANTASY AND SCIENCE FICTION

The modern fantasy and science fiction categories include books that depart from reality in a variety of ways: animals may talk, characters may move through time and space in magical ways, and some of the characters may be monsters or creatures that do not exist in real life. Science fiction is modern fantasy that uses technology, machines, robots, and computers to replace magic wands and special powers. These books appeal to the particularly vivid imagination of children in the elementary grades and lend themselves to delightful, creative extension activities.

	Type of entry	Grade level	Culture
Alexander, Lloyd. *Taran Wanderer.* Holt, 1967. This fourth book about the magical kingdom of Prydain recounts the experiences of Pig-Keeper Taran during his quest to learn the truth about himself.	E	6–8	
Andersen, Hans Christian. *The Emperor's New Clothes.* Retold and illustrated by Anne Rockwell. Crowell, 1982. This story is about a vain emperor's experiences with two very deceitful tailors.	E	4–8	
Andersen, Hans Christian. *The Nightingale.* Translated by Eva Le Gallienne and illustrated by Nancy Ekholm Burkert. Harper Junior Books, 1985. The little bird, though banished by the emperor in preference to a jeweled, mechanical imitation, remains faithful. When the emperor is near death, the little bird returns to help him.	C	4–8	
Andersen, Hans Christian. *The Ugly Duckling.* Retold and illustrated by Lorinda B. Cauley. Harcourt, 1979. When ostracized by the barnyard animals, the ugly duckling spends an unhappy year until he grows into a beautiful swan.	C	2–6	
Aruego, José, and Ariane Dewey. *We Hide, You Seek.* Greenwillow, 1979. Young readers are invited to find animals hidden in their natural habitat portrayed in the illustrations.	E	K–2	
Babbitt, Natalie. *Tuck Everlasting.* Farrar, 1975. The Tuck family faces an agonizing situation when they find out that a ten-year-old girl and an evil stranger share their secret.	E	6–8	
Bond, Michael. *A Bear Called Paddington.* Illustrated by Peggy Fortnum. Houghton, 1960. When Mr. and Mrs. Brown find a small bear at Paddington Station, he becomes one of the family.	E	4–6	

	Type of entry	Grade level	Culture
Cameron, Eleanor. *The Court of the Stone Children.* Avon, 1976. Nina solves a murder mystery that has been unsolved since the time of Napoleon. She is able to do this work with the help of a journal kept by a young woman in nineteenth-century France.	C	5–6	
Christopher, John. *The City of Gold and Lead.* Macmillan, 1967. This sequel to *The White Mountains* tells of three boys who set out on a secret mission to penetrate the City of the Tripods.	E	5–8	
Clark, Ann Nolan. *Year Walk.* Viking, 1975. A sixteen-year-old boy, in 1910, comes from the Basque country in Spain to Idaho to help his godfather herd sheep across the northwest frontier.	E	2–4	H
Coville, Bruce, and Katherine Coville. *Sarah's Unicorn.* Lippincott, 1979. Sarah's Aunt Mag is a good witch until an experiment turns her into an evil one. Sarah, with the aid of the magical powers of a unicorn, breaks the evil spell holding Aunt Mag.	E	1–3	
Dahl, Roald. *James and the Giant Peach.* Illustrated by Nancy Ekholm Burkert. Knopf, 1961. An adventure story about James and the animals he meets while trying to get away from his two aunts, Aunt Sponge and Aunt Spiker.	C	4–6	
Daugherty, James. *Andy and the Lion.* Viking, 1938. Andy reads a book about lions and then meets one with a thorn in its paw. The next time Andy sees the lion is at the circus. The lion escapes from its cage and frightens the viewers, but Andy, recognizing the lion, calms him, thereby saving the audience.	E	2–5	
Du Bois, William P. *Lion.* Viking, 1955. This fable is about an artist who invents an animal and calls it "Lion."	C	5–6	
Freeman, Don. *Bearymore.* Viking, 1976. A circus bear learns a new act in order to keep his job.	E	K–3	
Freeman, Don. *Dandelion.* Viking, 1964. Dandelion is invited to a tea and decides to wear a fancy outfit. Jennifer Giraffe does not recognize him and closes the door in his face. A subsequent rainstorm takes care of Dandelion's plight.	E	K–2	
Grahame, Kenneth. *The Wind in the Willows.* Illustrated by E. H. Shepard. Scribner, 1908. Three great friends, Mr. Rat, Mr. Mole, and Mr. Toad, share the life and habitat of each other in a most humorous manner.	E	5–7	
Han, Mieko. *Turtle Power—Vietnamese.* National Asian Center for Bilingual Education, 1983. Each page of this folktale from Vietnam is in both English and Vietnamese. A turtle saves the life of the Dragon King that lives in the sea. He uses ginseng.	C	1–6	V

	Type of entry	Grade level	Culture

Hunter, Mollie. *A Stranger Came Ashore.* Harper Junior Books, 1975. — E — 5–8

A young man who supposedly survived a shipwreck is offered shelter by the Hendersons. They learn firsthand of the haunting power of certain creatures called "Silkies" in this Shetland Island folktale.

Jarrell, Randall. *The Animal Family.* Random House, 1965. — E — 5–6

A lonely hunter befriends a curious mermaid. Through their years together, they befriend a bear cub, a baby lynx, and a shipwrecked baby boy.

Juster, Norton. *The Phantom Tollbooth.* Illustrated by Jules Feiffer. Random House, 1961. — E — 5–7

Milo, a lazy boy, journeys to a strange land to learn the importance of words and numbers, patience, and responsibility. His learning cures his boredom and lack of initiative.

Kellogg, Steven. *Island of the Skog.* Dial Books, 1973. — E — 3–4

A group of mice sets out to escape a cat. The mice land on an island inhabited by the Skog, a fearful monster.

Lawson, Robert. *Ben and Me.* Little, 1939. — C — 5–6

The story of Benjamin Franklin is told by Amos, a mouse that lives in Ben's fur cap. In this historical spoof, it is the mice that invent the Franklin stove, lightning rods, and discover the importance of lightning. They even write, "When in the course of human events . . ." and direct the course of American history while Franklin is in France.

Lawson, Robert. *Rabbit Hill.* Viking, 1944. — E — 5–6

All the animals were buzzing with the "news." New folks were coming—moving into the house! This is a warm story of the happenings that followed and the warm association that developed between animals and people.

L'Engle, Madeleine. *A Wrinkle in Time.* Farrar, 1962. — C — 5–6

A search for their missing scientist father takes two children through a science fiction fantasy in space and time with a vivid struggle between good and evil. The value of a close, loving family is emphasized.

Lewis, C. S. *The Lion, the Witch and the Wardrobe.* Illustrated by Pauline Baynes. Macmillan, 1950. — C — 5–6

Four English children adventure through an old wardrobe to enter the world of Narnia. They become kings and queens and find themselves in an endless conflict between good and evil, portrayed by a worthy lion and a malicious witch.

Lionni, Leo. *Alexander and the Wind-up Mouse.* Pantheon, 1969. — C — 1–3

Alexander, a real mouse, makes friends with Willy, a toy mouse, and wants to be just like him. When he discovers that Willy is to be thrown away, he changes his mind. This book has delightful illustrations made with a rice-paper collage technique.

	Type of entry	Grade level	Culture

Lobel, Arnold. *Fables.* Harper Junior Books, 1980.

C · **3–5**

The author presents 20 original fables about an assortment of animal characters from crocodile to ostrich.

Lobel, Arnold. *Frog and Toad Are Friends.* Harper Junior Books, 1970.

C · **K–3**

Five tales about the adventures of two best friends are presented with humor, style, and distinctive animal illustrations. Frog and Toad quarrel, make up, share, plan projects, and have fun in this easy-reading book.

Mayer, Mercer. *There's a Nightmare in My Closet.* Dial Books, 1968.

E · **K–4**

A small boy conquers his fear of the dark by letting his nightmare (a big, ugly monster) out of the closet and shooting it with his popgun.

Milne, A. A. *Winnie-the-Pooh.* Dutton, 1961; Dell, 1970.

C · **3–4**

This is a story of Christopher Robin and his toys that seem real to him. Kanga, Roo, Piglet, and Winnie-the-Pooh talk and play with Christopher in his games of make-believe.

Norton, Mary. *The Borrowers.* Harcourt, 1953; Voyager, 1965.

E · **4–6**

In this fantasy a tiny family lives beneath the floor of an old English country home and "borrows" things from the larger human residents.

O'Brien, Robert C. *Mrs. Frisby and the Rats of Nimh.* Atheneum, 1971; Aladdin-Atheneum, 1971.

E · **5–7**

This is a story of a widowed mouse and rats that have escaped from a Nimh laboratory after being taught to read. The rats help Mrs. Frisby, and she helps them.

Peet, Bill. *Big Bad Bruce.* Houghton, 1977.

C · **K–3**

Bruce, a great shaggy bear, terrorizes the other animals in the forest until one day, his rock-rolling fun is stopped by a crafty witch who reduces him in size so that he will get a taste of his own medicine.

Piper, Watty. *The Little Engine That Could.* Illustrated by George Hauman and Doris Hauman. Platt and Munk, 1961; Putnam, 1984.

E · **K–3**

The little engine does not make excuses when asked to help a tired engine. She hitches herself to the train, begins to tug and pull, and encourages herself with the familiar words, "I think I can, I think I can . . . I can, I think I can."

Rodgers, Mary. *Freaky Friday.* Harper Junior Books, 1972.

E · **5–7**

Annabel Andrews, thirteen, wakes up one morning and discovers that her mind is in her mother's body. She thinks the change-about is terrific, but she realizes as the day goes on that she is not able to cope with the events that surround her "husband," "daughter," and "son."

	Type of entry	Grade level	Culture

Selden, George. *Cricket in Times Square.* Illustrated by Garth Williams. Dell, 1970. — E, 5–6

Chester, the cricket, lives in a newsstand in Times Square. He has many adventures which climax with the rescue of the newsstand owner from financial disaster.

Sendak, Maurice. *Where the Wild Things Are.* Harper Junior Books, 1963. — C, K–5

Max's imagination changes his room into a forest near an ocean. In his boat he sails away to where the wild things are. He tames the terrible monsters, is made their king, and romps with them; but he feels lonely. He wants someone who loves him best. He returns to his very own room and his hot supper.

Seuss, Dr. (Theodore Geisel). *And to Think That I Saw It on Mulberry Street.* Vanguard, 1937. — C, K–3

A boy's imagination makes his walk home from school an exciting adventure as he sees chariots, elephants, bands, and much, much more.

Seuss, Dr. *The Cat in the Hat.* Random House, 1957. — E, K–3

Sally and her brother are home alone on a rainy day with nothing to do. The Cat in the Hat suddenly appears, full of mischief and tricks. He turns the house upside down.

Seuss, Dr. *Five Hundred Hats of Bartholomew Cubbins.* Vanguard, 1938. — C, 2–4

Bartholomew doffs his hat before the king only to discover another hat has appeared on his head. The king is furious and condemns Bartholomew to death. As he madly pulls hats off, he is led to the highest tower. The hats begin to change. The five-hundredth hat is more glorious than the king's crown, so the king spares Bartholomew's life.

Steig, William. *Abel's Island.* Farrar, 1976. — C, 4–6

The author describes a gentleman mouse that has been lazy and pampered until stranded on an island. The mouse learns to cope with solitude, finding food and shelter before he returns from the island a year later.

Steig, William. *Sylvester and the Magic Pebble.* Simon and Schuster, 1969; Windmill Books, 1969. — C, 1–3

Sylvester, a young donkey, finds a magic pebble and turns himself into a rock when a hungry lion appears.

Turkle, Brinton. *Do Not Open.* Dutton, 1981. — C, 3–6

Miss Moody, a lifelong beachcomber, finds a mysterious bottle marked "Do Not Open," but she does, and a terrible monster emerges. Miss Moody is not frightened, though, and the situation is happily resolved.

Van Allsburg, Chris. *Jumanji.* Houghton, 1981. — C, 4–6

A brother and sister left at home alone for an afternoon are bored until they find a mysterious game that warns, "If you start, you have to finish." As each jungle animal on the game board is reached, the animal comes alive in the apartment. The children learn to cooperate to finish the game.

STORYTELLING CAN MOTIVATE CHILDREN TO READ, AS WELL AS INTRODUCING THEM TO CULTURAL VALUES AND LITERARY TRADITIONS.

	Type of entry	Grade level	Culture

Van Leeuwen, Jean. *Tales of Oliver Pig.* Dial Books, 1979.

  The author presents five tales about Oliver's life at home with a loving Father, Mother Pig, and little sister Amanda.

E — 1–4

White, E. B. *Charlotte's Web.* Illustrated by Garth Williams. Harper Junior Books, 1952.

  The author presents a touching story of a young pig named Wilbur and his spider friend Charlotte. The theme of friendship is carefully developed throughout the story.

C — 4–6

White, E. B. *Stuart Little.* Harper Junior Books, 1945.

  Stuart is an unusual person—being no bigger than a mouse at birth. This is a chronicle of his interesting life and adventures.

E — 4–6

Williams, Jay. *Everyone Knows What a Dragon Looks Like.* Four Winds Press, 1976.

  A fat, bald, old man appears one day in a city on the Chinese border and announces that he is a dragon. No one believes him until he becomes a mighty wind and drives off their enemy.

E — 3–6

Williams, Jay. *The Practical Princess and Other Stories.* Parents Magazine Press, 1978.

  Six clever girls outsmart, outdo, and outthink a few "lollygagging" males.

E — 4–6

Williams, Margery. *The Velveteen Rabbit.* Doubleday, 1958.

  This magical fable is about a toy rabbit that becomes a real rabbit with the help of a boy who loves it.

C — 3–6

Wiseman, David. *Jeremy Visick.* Houghton, 1981.

  When Matthew learns how Jeremy died in the Wheal Maid Mine, he narrowly escapes death himself, but he brings peace to Jeremy's ghost.

E — 5–6

Yashima, Mitsu, and Taro Yashima. *Momo's Kitten.* Viking, 1961; Penguin, 1977.

  A little Japanese-American girl, Momo, finds a stray kitten (a Nyan-Nyan in Japanese). Nyan-Nyan has babies, and Momo finds homes for them.

C — K–3 — J

Zolotow, Charlotte. *Mr. Rabbit and the Lovely Present.* Harper Junior Books, 1962.

  After a day of searching, a serious little girl and a tall, white rabbit decide on a basket of fruit as a gift for the girl's mother.

C — K–3

CHILDREN IMPROVE

THEIR READING ABILITY

BY READING A LOT.

POETRY

oetry is a unique literary form. It derives power and meaning through an economy of language—"the best words in the best order." Poetry should be heard as well as seen, it should be read aloud, and it should be experienced.

The books listed below are intended as resources for providing poetic experiences. Most are collections chosen to give teachers and students opportunities to browse and select both new and familiar poems to sample and share. The books represent all forms of poetry: narrative, lyric, ballad, haiku, limerick, concrete poems, and free verse. The ethnic and cultural voices and styles of many people are reflected.

Some anthologies contain poems by a single author, while others are collections of the works of many poets. Many works are illustrated creatively to extend the reader's understanding and enjoyment. Some of the collections contain poems that span a wide range of reading, interest, and response levels.

The variety of works suggested should allow teachers to present poetry naturally and regularly so that it can become a meaningful, relevant, and pleasurable part of each student's life.

	Type of entry	Grade level	Culture
Adoff, Arnold. *All the Colors of the Race.* Illustrated by John Steptoe. Lothrop, 1982. The poems in this book are written from the point of view of a child with a black mother and a white father.	E	4–6	B
Adoff, Arnold. *Black Is Brown Is Tan.* Illustrated by Emily Arnold McCully. Harper Junior Books, 1973. These poems are about a family with a white father and a black mother. They enjoy being together doing family-type things.	E	5–6	B
Adoff, Arnold. *Outside-Inside Poems.* Illustrated by John Steptoe. Lothrop, 1981. These poems are about experiences such as standing in baseball shoes or expressing one's inside thoughts and feelings about being young and growing. The drawings are in black and white.	C	1–3	B
Aldis, Dorothy. *All Together.* Putnam, 1925, 1952. These poems are about all sorts of human/child experiences, from radiator lions to flies to going to sleep.	E	K–4	
America Forever New: A Book of Poems. Edited by Sara Brewton and John Brewton. Crowell, 1968. This collection includes poems about American history, tall tales, pioneers, city dwellers, and landscapes of America.	C	2–6	

	Type of entry	Grade level	Culture

Amon, Aline. *The Earth Is Sore: Native Americans on Nature.* Illustrated by Aline Amon. Atheneum, 1981. — C | K–6 | I

These poems and songs express the feelings and thoughts of American Indians about nature, the white man, land misuse, and a desire to return again to a respect for life. Information about the tribe whose thoughts are expressed is presented with each entry.

Baylor, Byrd. *When Clay Sings* (Southwest). Scribner, 1972. — C | 3–4 | I

Poems and drawings describe the life of the American Indian in earlier times as depicted on pottery.

Benet, Rosemary, and Stephen Vincent Benet. *A Book of Americans.* Rinehart, 1933. — C | 3–6

Poems about famous Americans are presented chronologically.

Black Out Loud. Edited by Arnold Adoff. Macmillan, 1970. — E | 5–8 | B

This anthology of modern poems by black Americans covers a broad range of topics—from being black to Martin Luther King, Jr., to being a poet.

Bodecker, N. M. *Hurry, Hurry, Mary Dear! And Other Nonsense.* Atheneum, 1976. — E | 2–5

This is a collection of happy nonsense and tongue-twisting poetry.

A Book of Animal Poems. Selected by William Cole. Viking, 1973. — C | 2–6

This book contains approximately 250 poems written by traditional and modern poets. The poems are about all kinds of common and exotic animals.

Brooks, Gwendolyn. *Bronzeville Boys and Girls.* Harper Junior Books, 1956. — E | 2–6 | B

These poems are set in Chicago, but they describe what it is like to live in a big city anywhere. The name of a child is used as the title of each poem.

Ciardi, John. *You Read to Me, I'll Read to You.* Illustrated by Edward Gorey. Lippincott, 1962. — E | 1–3

These are humorous poems that children might experience or think about. Examples range from "Daddy fixing breakfast" to "What to do when one meets a tiger."

Crazy to Be Alive in Such a Strange World. Edited by Nancy Larrick. Lippincott, 1977. — C | 3–6

This book includes poetic portraits done by well-known and unknown poets. Some of the material was taken from high school publications. The moods and subjects are varied.

Cricket Songs: Japanese Haiku. Translated by Harry Behn. Harcourt, 1964. — C | 3–6

Brief, nonrhyming poems express the wonders of nature.

	Type of entry	Grade level	Culture

Dickinson, Emily. *I'm Nobody! Who Are You? The Poems of Emily Dickinson.* Stemmer House, 1978. — E, 5–6

This is a collection of poems by Emily Dickinson. An explanation of the poems is presented at the front of the book.

Fisher, Aileen. *Out in the Dark and Daylight.* Harper Junior Books, 1980. — C, 2–6

This collection of poems celebrates all the small things that make up each day.

Froman, Robert. *Seeing Things: A Book of Poems.* Harper Junior Books, 1974. — C, 4–6

The words of these 51 brief poems are arranged on the pages in shapes appropriate to the subject of the poem.

Froman, Robert. *Street Poems.* McCall, 1971. — E, 4–6

These poems have been written especially for city children. The author plays with shapes in this book so that the print emphasizes the message of the words.

The Gift Outright: America to Her Poets. Edited by Helen Plotz. Greenwillow, 1977. — C, 4–8

Poems of science and mathematics are illustrated with wood carvings by Clara Leighton.

Greenfield, Eloise. *Honey I Love: And Other Love Poems.* Harper Junior Books, 1978. — E, 3–8, B

The poems in this book are about things that are loved. They include "I look pretty," "fun," "riding on the train," "Harriet Tubman," and "by myself."

Hopkins, Lee Bennett. *The Sky Is Full of Song.* Harper Junior Books, 1983. — E, 1–3

The 38 short poems in this book are designed to capture the mood of each season. Numerous outstanding poets are represented.

How to Eat a Poem and Other Morsels. Selected by Rose Agree. Pantheon Books, 1967. — C, 3–6

These poems are about food and eating (for example, "How to Eat Poetry" and "How to Eat a Dragon").

Howard, Coralie. *The First Book of Short Verse.* Watts, 1964. — C, 2–6

This book contains short poems by Frost and Sandburg in addition to poems by children. It includes an introduction on "why people write poetry."

Hughes, Langston. *Don't You Turn Back.* Edited by Lee Bennett Hopkins. Knopf, 1969. — E, 5–8

The poems of protest in this collection deal primarily with racial pride and human needs.

Hughes, Langston. *The Dream Keeper.* Knopf, 1945. — C, 4–8

Many of the poems in this volume show the validity of the blues as a poetic form.

THERE IS NO SUBSTITUTE FOR A TEACHER WHO READS CHILDREN GOOD STORIES.

	Type of entry	Grade level	Culture
In the Trail of the Wind: American Indian Poems and Ritual Orations. Edited by John Bierhorst. Farrar, 1972. These poems represent the best known Indian cultures of North and South America. Included are omens, battle songs, orations, love lyrics, prayers, dreams, and incantations.	E	5–8	I
Knock at a Star: A Child's Introduction to Poetry. Edited by X. J. Kennedy and Dorothy Kennedy. Little, 1982. This is an appealing collection of American and English poetry.	C	3–8	
Lear, Edward. ***How Pleasant to Know Mr. Lear!*** Holiday House, 1982. This is a collection of nonsense verse with the author's own illustrations.	C	4–6	
Listen, Children, Listen: An Anthology of Poems for the Very Young. Edited by Myra C. Livingston and illustrated by Trina Schart Hyman. Harcourt, 1972. This is a collection of poems about the moods and interests of young children.	C	K–3	
Livingston, Myra C. ***Circle of Seasons.*** Holiday House, 1982. The four seasons are revealed in a blend of poetry and paintings.	C	2–4	
McCord, David. ***One at a Time.*** Little, 1977. This book includes selections of short poems about everyday topics such as insects, picket fences, and tree climbing.	C	2–6	
Merriam, Eve. ***Independent Voices.*** Illustrated by Arvis Stewart. Atheneum, 1968. These poems feature Benjamin Franklin, Elizabeth Blackwell, Frederick Douglass, Henry Thoreau, Lucretia Mott, Ida B. Wells, and others.	E	1–3	
Merriam, Eve. ***There Is No Rhyme for Silver.*** Atheneum, 1962. In these poems for children, the poet uses small, exciting words that stimulate the senses.	C	3–6	
Moore, Lilian. ***Something New Begins.*** Atheneum, 1982. Selected poems are grouped under seven headings in which the poet has used vivid imagery and infectious humor.	C	3–6	
My Song Is a Piece of Jade: Poems of Ancient Mexico in English and Spanish. Edited by Toni de Gerez. Little, 1984. This book includes unrhymed poems, printed in both English and Spanish, of songs and singer, artist, storyteller, and doctor. There are many comparisons with birds and plants.	C	3–6	H
My Tang's Tungled and Other Ridiculous Situations. Compiled by Sara Brewton. Crowell, 1973. This book is a collection of tongue twisters and short, humorous verses by many well-known writers.	C	2–6	

	Type of entry	Grade level	Culture
O'Neill, Mary. *Hailstones and Halibut Bones.* Illustrated by Leonard Weisgard. Doubleday, 1961.	C	3–6	

The author introduces color through her use of a series of clever poems and illustrations.

	Type of entry	Grade level	Culture
Oxford Book of Poetry for Children. Edited by Edward Blishen. Watts, 1963.	E	6–8	

This collection of poems introduces verse to younger children to help them make the transition from nursery rhymes to more serious poetry.

	Type of entry	Grade level	Culture
Piping Down the Valleys Wild. Edited by Nancy Larrick. Delacorte, 1968.	C	3–6	

This poetry anthology contains works ranging from old folk songs and classical English poems to the works of modern poets. Each of the 16 sections deals with a particular subject: time of day, event, experience, and so forth.

	Type of entry	Grade level	Culture
Poem Stew. Edited by William Cole and illustrated by Karen Ann Weinhaus. Lippincott, 1981.	C	5–6	

This is a collection of funny poems about food. Subjects vary from a Thanksgiving dinner from a turkey's point of view to a look at hot cocoa left too long to cool.

	Type of entry	Grade level	Culture
Poetry of Earth and Sky. Illustrated by Adrienne Adams. Scribner, 1972.	E	4–8	

This collection of poetry by well-known poets is about animals, nature, and the sky.

	Type of entry	Grade level	Culture
Pomerantz, Charlotte. *If I Had a Paka: Poems in Eleven Languages.* Illustrated by Nancy Tafuri. Greenwillow, 1982.	E	K–5	

This collection of poetry represents a variety of cultures. They include words and phrases from 11 languages (for example, Serbo-Croatian, Swahili, and Vietnamese).

	Type of entry	Grade level	Culture
Prelutsky, Jack. *The New Kid on the Block.* Greenwillow, 1984.	E	3–6	

This book of humorous poems for young people contains more than 100 poems with subjects ranging from jellyfish stew to a wolf at the laundromat.

	Type of entry	Grade level	Culture
The Ring in the Prairie. Edited by John Bierhorst. Dial Books, 1970.	E	4–6	I

This romantic Shawnee Indian legend is about a young hunter who discovers a strange circle worn in the prairie grass from the dancing of 12 beautiful sisters who come down from the sky.

	Type of entry	Grade level	Culture
Sandburg, Carl. *Rainbows Are Made: Poems by Carl Sandburg.* Harcourt, 1982.	E	6–8	

This excellent anthology contains 70 of the poet's early poems. They represent a wide spectrum of subjects from "Pencils" to "River Moons."

	Type of entry	Grade level	Culture
Starbird, Kaye. *The Covered Bridge House and Other Poems.* Illustrated by Jim Arnosky. Four Winds Press, 1979.	E	5–8	

The 35 poems in this collection are about children and their perceptions, experiences, heightened awarenesses, and responses.

Strings: A Gathering of Family Poems. Edited by Paul B. Janeczko. Bradbury Press, 1984.	E	5–6	

This book presents poetry about family relationships and experiences: as parents, children, brother and sister, husband and wife, niece and nephew, and grandchildren. More than 100 poems are included.

Surprises. Edited by Lee Bennett Hopkins. Harper Junior Books, 1984.	C	2–3	

Imaginative and fun-filled poems have been grouped into sections about boats, trains, planes, rain, sun, snow, and good-night feelings.

Sutherland, Zena, and Myra Livingston. *The Scott, Foresman Anthology of Children's Literature.* Scott, Foresman, 1984.	C	2–6	

This anthology presents nursery rhymes, poetry, folk literature, fantasy and realistic fiction, historical fiction and biography, and nonfiction. It also includes a bibliography of major books.

The Trees Stand Shining: Poetry of the North American Indian. Selected by Hettie Jones and illustrated by Robert Andrew Parker. Dial, 1971.	E	5–8	I

Each of these short, unrhymed lyrics is ascribed to a particular tribe. Included are prayers and observations of weather and animal life. One poem is a sad description of Indian-white relations.

Tripp, Wallace. *A Great Big Ugly Man Came Up and Tied His Horse to Me: A Book of Nonsense Verse.* Little, 1973.	C	3–6	

This is a collection of silly, funny, and clever as well as mischievous poems (for example, "A horse who thought he was a fly, an old man eating his shoe, and the one who came up and tied his horse to me!").

READING . . . IS NOT SOMETHING THAT IS MASTERED ONCE. RATHER, IT IS A SKILL THAT CONTINUES TO IMPROVE THROUGH PRACTICE.

CONTEMPORARY REALISTIC FICTION

This category consists of stories about children, adults, and animals that are set in modern times with events that could happen. The stories help children understand themselves and others by showing that other people have thoughts, feelings, problems, and experiences similar to their own. Many of the stories can help children feel more comfortable in dealing with difficult situations.

Contemporary realistic fiction includes works that have the following characteristics: (1) the theme is significant and makes an impression on the reader; (2) the plot is a true-to-life portrayal of events and feelings of contemporary people; (3) the character's personality is fully developed; and (4) the language reflects the language of the times.

	Type of entry	Grade level	Culture
Atkinson, Mary. *Maria Teresa.* Lollipop Power, 1979. A contemporary story of a young Chicano girl who moves to a small midwestern town. She is immediately faced, for the first time in her life, with discrimination. Her puppet, Monteja, helps in an appreciable way.	C	3–6	H
Bourne, Miriam Anne. *Emilio's Summer Day.* Harper and Row, 1966. Emilio spends a hot day in his urban neighborhood. The best part of the day is when the children play in the spray from the water truck.	E	2–4	
Bulla, Clyde Robert. *Shoeshine Girl.* Harper Junior Books, 1975. Ten-year-old Sarah Ida has been sent to her aunt's home for the summer. Determined to get some money, Sarah Ida gets a job at a shoeshine stand.	E	3–5	
Bunting, Eve. *The Happy Funeral.* Harper Junior Books, 1982. A young Chinese-American girl's grandfather dies. The family observes many traditional customs and remembers happy experiences.	E	5–6	C
Bunting, Eve. *Someone Is Hiding on Alcatraz Island.* Houghton, 1984. Danny saw a mugging and reported it. Now the outlaws, a gang from Danny's school, are out to get him. The outlaws trap Danny and a park service employee in a prison block on Alcatraz.	E	5–6	
Burch, Robert. *Queenie Peavy.* Illustrated by Jerry Lazare. Viking, 1966. The 1930s in Georgia were hard, especially for thirteen-year-old Queenie Peavy. Her adored father was in jail and she had few friends at school, but she also had strength and courage when things got even worse.	C	5–6	

	Type of entry	Grade level	Culture

Byars, Betsy C. *The Summer of the Swans.* Illustrated by Ted Coconis. Viking, 1970. — C — 5–8

Sara, jolted out of a period of discontent by the disappearance of her retarded ten-year-old brother, finds herself through her successful search for him.

Cleary, Beverly. *Dear Mr. Henshaw.* Morrow, 1983. — C — 5–7

Leigh Botts, now a sixth grader, began writing to his favorite author, Boyd Henshaw, in the second grade. The reader learns how Leigh adjusts to new situations (for example, the absence of his father).

Cleary, Beverly. *Ramona and Her Father.* Illustrated by Alan Tiegreen. Morrow, 1977. — C — 3–5

The family routine is upset during Ramona's year in second grade when her father unexpectedly loses his job.

Cohen, Barbara. *Thank You, Jackie Robinson.* Lothrop, 1974. — E — 5–7 — B

Davy, a black cook in Sam's mother's restaurant, has taken the fatherless boy to many baseball games. When Davy has a heart attack, Sam gets an autographed baseball for him from Jackie Robinson.

DePaola, Tomie. *Nana Upstairs and Nana Downstairs.* Putnam, 1973. — C — 2–4

The story describes Tommy's companionable Sunday visits with his grandmother and his invalid great-grandmother, as well as his first experience with death when the latter dies.

De Saint-Exupery, Antoine. *The Little Prince.* Harcourt, 1943. — C — 2–8

A flier makes a forced landing in the Sahara Desert. He meets Little Prince from Asteroid B612 who tells the flier of his many experiences on other planets.

Dunnahoo, Terry. *Who Needs Espie Sanchez?* Dutton, 1977. — E — 4–7

Espie Sanchez's curiosity is aroused by a young wealthy girl who befriends her after both are involved in a tragic traffic accident.

Enright, Elizabeth. *Thimble Summer.* Holt, 1938. — E — 4–5

This is a well-illustrated story of the day-to-day experiences of life on a Wisconsin farm and of Garnet's "good luck" thimble that she found.

Estes, Eleanor. *The Hundred Dresses.* Harcourt, 1944. — C — 3–6

When Wanda moves away, snubbed and unhappy, leaving pictures of her dream dresses behind for a contest, her classmates realize how cruel they had been to the deaf girl.

Estes, Eleanor. *The Moffats.* Illustrated by Louis Slobodkin. Harcourt, 1941. — E — 3–6

The reader sees a family, not poverty-stricken but poor, of four young Moffats from five to fifteen years of age and their Mama through the eyes of nine-year-old Janey.

	Type of entry	Grade level	Culture

Fitzgerald, John D. *The Great Brain.* Dial Books, 1967.

    This autobiographical yarn about Tom Fitzgerald was spun by his brother John, age seven, who tells stories about himself and his family with considerable imagination.

(E, 5–6)

Fitzhugh, Louise. *Harriet the Spy.* Harper Junior Books, 1964.

    After getting into difficulty because of her writing and spying and a boring stay at home, Harriet talks to a psychiatrist, who convinces her to channel her abilities along more constructive lines.

(E, 5–6)

Fox, Paula. *One-Eyed Cat.* Bradbury, 1984.

    An eleven-year-old shoots a stray cat with his new air rifle, subsequently suffers from guilt, and eventually assumes responsibility for it.

(C, 6)

Galbraith, Claire K. *Victor.* Illustrated by Bill Commerford. Little, 1971.

    Victor, a Mexican-American boy, hates school because he cannot understand his teacher well enough to know what is expected of him. In frustration he lashes out at his mother. The result is the core of the book.

(C, 2–5, H)

Gates, Doris. *Blue Willow.* Viking, 1940.

    Janey and her precious blue willow plate are always moving so her father can find work. Finally she finds a friend and, after many adventures, a settled home as well.

(C, 4–5, H)

Gipson, Fred. *Old Yeller.* Illustrated by Carl Burger. Harper Junior Books, 1956.

    This story of a boy's relationship with his dog on a farm in the late 1860s is a tale of a dog's devotion to its duty and its master.

(E, 5–8)

Greene, Bette. *Philip Hall Likes Me, I Reckon Maybe.* Dial Books, 1974.

    This is a story of the adventures of Bette, a bright and lively black girl whose only real problems result from her infatuation with a boy from the next farm.

(C, 4–6, B)

Greene, Bette. *Summer of My German Soldier.* Dial Books, 1973.

    Patty, a lonely, misunderstood twelve-year-old, hides an escaped German prisoner of war. He is found and killed. Patty's family loses everything, and she is sent to reform school.

(E, 6–8)

Greenfield, Eloise. *Sister.* Crowell, 1974.

    A thirteen-year-old black girl who fears she will drift away from her mother, as her older sister has, finds herself while reading her sister's diary.

(E, 6–8, B)

Hahn, Jae Hyun. *Seven Korean Sisters.* The Institute for Intercultural Studies, Los Angeles, 1980.

    The origin of the sakdong chogori worn by Korean girls and women on special days is explained in this fanciful story.

(C, 1–5, K)

	Type of entry	Grade level	Culture

Hahn, Jae Hyun, and Han Hahn. ***Special Korean Birthday.*** The Institute for Intercultural Studies, Los Angeles, 1980.

Young Soo, a Korean immigrant boy, invites his friend Paul to his baby sister's first birthday party. The sister receives many gifts and is seated at her birthday table with the objects and food. Paul comes to understand the significance of the gifts and to appreciate his friend's Korean heritage.

C 1–3 K

Hamilton, Virginia. ***The House of Dies Drear.*** Macmillan, 1968.

This story, seen through the eyes of Thomas, a young black boy, unravels the mystery of an enormous old house in a southern Ohio town. It had once played an important part in the Underground Railway.

C 5–6 B

Hamilton, Virginia. ***Zeely.*** Macmillan, 1967.

A city child who spends a summer on a farm fantasizes about her mysterious neighbor who looks like a Watusi queen.

C 4–6 B

Henry, Marguerite. ***King of the Wind.*** Illustrated by Wesley Dennis. Rand, 1948.

The story of an Arab stable boy's love for a sultan's horse that began the line of thoroughbreds from which Man O' War was sired.

E 5–6

Holman, Felice. ***Slake's Limbo.*** Dial Books, 1975.

Aremis Slake, a fifteen-year-old boy totally alone, finds refuge in the New York City subway system when he discovers a hidden construction site in the shape of a cave. He learns to survive on his own, makes important discoveries about himself, and ultimately is accepted.

E 5–6

Ishigo, Estelle. ***Lone Heart Mountain.*** Publisher not identified, 1982.

This is a story of the Japanese-American relocation camp in Wyoming during the days of World War II.

E 6–8 J

Jukes, Mavis. ***Like Jake and Me.*** Knopf, 1984.

Alex feels that he does not have much in common with his stepfather, Jake, until a fuzzy brown spider brings them together.

E 4–6

Konigsburg, E. L. ***From the Mixed-Up Files of Mrs. Basil E. Frankweiler.*** Atheneum, 1967.

Claudia decides to run away because she is not appreciated at home. She enjoys luxury; so, she chooses the Metropolitan Museum of Art as her hiding place. With her brother, she tries to unravel a mystery to make herself important.

C 5–6

Konigsburg. E. L. ***Jennifer, Hecate, Macbeth, William McKinley, and Me, Elizabeth.*** Atheneum, 1967.

Elizabeth finds a new friend who is also a witch, and she agrees to take Elizabeth as an apprentice. Elizabeth discovers that Jennifer is also a girl who wants to have friends, and the witchcraft is not needed.

E 5–6

	Type of entry	Grade level	Culture

Krumgold, Joseph. *And Now Miguel.* Crowell, 1953.

A wish dominates Miguel Chavez: that he may be allowed to go to the mountains with the men of the family and their herds. The wish comes true.

E 6–8 H

Lowry, Lois. *Anastasia Krupnik.* Bantam, 1981.

Anastasia is coping with being an only child, living with her professor father and artist mother, and making lists, when she discovers that her mother is expecting a baby. She tries to think of a terrible name.

C 4–6

MacLachlan, Patricia. *Arthur, for the Very First Time.* Harper Junior Books, 1980.

Ten-year-old Arthur spends the summer with two relatives: an eccentric great-aunt and great-uncle.

C 4–6

Mathis, Sharon B. *The Hundred Penny Box.* Viking, 1975.

Michael's one-hundred-year-old great-great-aunt Dew lives mostly in the memories of her past, represented by the 100 pennies she keeps in a wooden box. Michael's mother struggles to convince aunt Dew to live in the present.

C 5–8 B

Maury, Inez. *My Mother the Mail Carrier.* Feminist Press, 1976.

Lupita describes her mother's job as a mail carrier and her own life in a one-parent family.

C 2–4 H

Miles, Miska. *Annie and the Old One.* Illustrated by Peter Parnall. Little, 1971.

Annie comes to accept the impending death of her grandmother as she recognizes the wonder of life.

C 2–8 I

Ness, Evaline. *Sam, Bangs, and Moonshine.* Harper Junior Books, 1966.

A small girl learns a near-tragic lesson in distinguishing fact from fantasy.

C 2–4

Paterson, Katherine. *Bridge to Terabithia.* Illustrated by Donna Diamond. Crowell, 1977; Avon, 1978.

Jess and Leslie become friends, even though Leslie beats him in a footrace at school. Together they reign supreme in a magical kingdom that Leslie creates until the tragedy of her death by drowning changes Jess forever. How Jess learns to cope with this tragedy, helped by the memory of Leslie, gives promise to his future.

C 5–8

Paterson, Katherine. *The Great Gilly Hopkins.* Crowell, 1978; Avon, 1978.

Gilly is a foster child who has been angry, lonely, and hurting for so long that she is always ready for a fight. She finds love in a foster home that gives her the strength to face tough days ahead.

E 5–8

Politi, Leo. *Mieko.* Golden Gate, 1969.

A Japanese-American girl living in Los Angeles feels that she must become Queen of the Nisei Week Festival to please her parents. "Little Tokyo" is beautifully pictured.

E 1–3 J

THE AMOUNT OF TIME CHILDREN SPEND READING IN THE AVERAGE CLASSROOM IS SMALL.

	Type of entry	Grade level	Culture

Rawls, Wilson. ***Where the Red Fern Grows.*** Doubleday, 1961. — C — 5–7

Looking back more than 50 years to his boyhood in the Ozarks, the author recalls how he achieved his heart's desire in the ownership of two hounds, how he taught them hunting, and how they won the championship coon hunt before Old Dan was killed by a mountain lion.

Sachs, Marilyn. ***The Bear's House.*** Doubleday, 1971. — E — 5–6

Although she sucks her thumb, smells bad, and loses herself in the make-believe world of the three bears' dollhouse, a fourth grader does know how to care for her baby sister.

Sonneborn, Ruth. ***Friday Night Is Papa Night.*** Viking, 1970. — E — 2–4 — H

Because Pedro's father is unable to come home during the week, each Friday night is a special occasion. One evening Papa does not come home, and the children are heartbroken. But when a weary Papa finally arrives in the middle of the night, everyone receives popsicles and presents.

Steptoe, John. ***Stevie.*** Harper Junior Books, 1969. — C — 2–3 — B

Robert, a small black boy, tells the story of an intruder, Stevie, who comes to stay at his house because both of his parents work. Stevie is a pest and wants everything he sees. After he leaves, the house is still, but there are memories of games played.

Taylor, Theodore. ***The Trouble with Tuck.*** Doubleday, 1981. — E — 6–8

A young girl trains her blind dog to follow and trust a seeing-eye companion dog. Helen does not give up until she has taken care of Tuck's problem.

Williams, Vera B. ***Chair for My Mother.*** Greenwillow, 1982. — C — 2–4

A little girl tells the story of living with odds and ends after her home is destroyed by fire. She dreams about a jar again being filled with coins so that a comfortable chair can be purchased for Mother, who comes home from work feeling very weary. The jar is filled, a chair is purchased, and all love the comfortable chair.

Wojciechowska, Maia. ***Shadow of a Bull.*** Illustrated by Alvin Smith. Atheneum, 1964. — E — 6–8

Ever since Manolo's father's death, the town has waited for Manolo to be old enough to follow in his father's footsteps as a bullfighter. Manolo works hard to face this moment with honor, knowing that it could bring his death.

Yarbrough, Camille. ***Cornrows.*** Putnam, 1979. — E — 3–6 — B

Storytelling time is a daily affair, and it is a time when children sit to have their hair braided. This is the time they hear the regal history of cornrowing and its meaning.

Yashima, Taro. ***Crow Boy.*** Viking, 1955. — C — 3–7 — J

A young boy from the mountain area in Japan goes to school in a nearby village where he is taunted by his classmates. When he feels rejected, an understanding teacher helps him gain acceptance. He is nicknamed "Crow Boy," because he can imitate a crow's caw.

	Type of entry	Grade level	Culture
Yep, Laurence. ***Child of the Owl.*** Harper, 1977.	C	6–8	C
Zolotow, Charlotte. ***My Grandson Lew.*** Harper, 1974.	C	K–3	

Yep, Laurence. ***Child of the Owl.*** Harper, 1977.
   The story is set in San Francisco's Chinatown where Casey, a young girl, must live with her grandmother because her father is a compulsive gambler. Grandmother tells her the legend of the owl spirit, which helps her realize that she may never feel completely at ease as a Chinese or an American; but she cannot cut herself off from her Chinese heritage.

Zolotow, Charlotte. ***My Grandson Lew.*** Harper, 1974.
   Lew and his mother recount images of Grandfather; this experience helps them feel less lonely after Grandfather's death.

HISTORICAL FICTION

History is made by people—what they did, what they said, and what they were—people with strengths and weaknesses who experienced victories and defeats. History becomes exciting for children when the people who made it seem to arise alive from the pages. Historical fiction adds the human dimension to the historical facts presented in textbooks and helps students view history as a story of life as it was lived by real people in the past.

Historical fiction, though it is set in a time prior to the one in which we live, is like contemporary realism in that it relates human experiences in the natural world. The historical novel is an imaginative story in which the author has deliberately reconstructed the life and times of a past period.

However, a book of historical fiction should do more than relate a good story of the past, authentically and imaginatively. It should illuminate the problems of today by examining those of yesterday. The themes of historical books are basic ones: the meaning of freedom, loyalty and treachery, love and hate, acceptance of new ways, closed minds versus open ones, and the age-old struggle between good and evil. A well-written work of historical fiction will have a universal and long-lasting impact on the lives of its readers.

	Type of entry	Grade level	Culture
Benchley, Nathaniel. ***George the Drummer Boy.*** Harper Junior Books, 1977.	E	4–5	

Benchley, Nathaniel. ***George the Drummer Boy.*** Harper Junior Books, 1977.
   This story describes incidents at Lexington and Concord as seen and recounted through the eyes of a British drummer boy.

	Type of entry	Grade level	Culture

Benchley, Nathaniel. *Sam the Minuteman.* Harper Junior Books, 1969.

This is an easy-to-read account of Sam and his father fighting as minutemen against the British at Lexington.

| | E | 4–5 | |

Brenner, Barbara. *Wagon Wheels.* Harper Junior Books, 1978.

After the Civil War a black family travels to Kansas to claim some free land offered through the Homestead Act.

| | C | 2–5 | B |

Brink, Carol R. *Caddie Woodlawn.* Illustrated by Trina Schart Hyman. Macmillan, 1973.

Caddie, an eleven-year-old tomboy, grows up in the mid-nineteenth century on the Wisconsin frontier.

| | E | 4–6 | |

Burchard, Peter. *Bimby.* Coward, 1968.

This story, set in Georgia just before the Civil War, is about one crucial day in the life of a young American slave. He risks his life for freedom.

| | E | 5–6 | B |

Byars, Betsy C. *Trouble River.* Viking, 1969.

A twelve-year-old boy builds a raft, but he has no idea that it will serve as a means of escape for him and his grandmother when hostile Indians threaten their cabin.

| | E | 5–8 | |

Clapp, Patricia. *I'm Deborah Sampson: A Soldier in the War of the Revolution.* Lothrop, 1977.

A woman disguises herself as a man in order to enlist and fight in the American Revolution.

| | C | 5–6 | |

Dalgliesh, Alice. *The Courage of Sarah Noble.* Illustrated by Leonard Weisgard. Scribner, 1954.

A young girl finds the courage to go alone with her father to build a new home in the wilderness and to stay alone with the Indians when her father goes to bring back the rest of the family.

| | C | 2–4 | |

DeJong, Meindert. *House of Sixty Fathers.* Harper Junior Books, 1956.

This is a vivid and realistic story of China during the early days of the Japanese invasion. The young Chinese boy, Tien Pao, was separated from his parents during a storm and swept downriver on a sampan.

| | E | 6 | C |

The Fall of the Aztecs. Edited by Shirley Glubok. St. Martin's Press, 1963.

This story is based on the conquest of Mexico, 1519—1549.

| | E | 4–6 | |

Fleischman, Sid. *By the Great Horn Spoon.* Little, 1963.

Jack's adventures begin when he and his aunt's butler stow away on a ship bound for California. The Gold Rush of 1849 is part of the adventure.

| | E | 5–6 | |

Fox, Paula. *Slave Dancer.* Bradbury, 1973.

A thirteen-year-old boy, kidnapped by the crew of an Africa-bound ship, is horrified to discover he is on a slaver. His job is to play music for the human cargo.

| | E | 5–8 | B |

	Type of entry	Grade level	Culture

Goble, Paul, and Dorothy Goble. ***Red Hawk's Account of Custer's Last Battle.*** Pantheon, 1969. — E · 5–8 · I

Custer's last stand at Little Big Horn is described as it might have been seen by one of the Indians in the battle.

Haley, Gail. ***Jack Jouett's Ride.*** Viking, 1973. — C · 3–5

The author describes an incident during the American Revolution when Jack Jouett rode to warn Thomas Jefferson of the coming of Tarleton's raiders.

Hall, Donald. ***The Ox-Cart Man.*** Illustrated by Barbara Cooney. Viking, 1978. — C · 3–4

This picture book shows the turn of the seasons in a New England village as a family makes things to sell at the Portsmouth Market.

Haugaard, Erik C. ***Hakon of Rogen's Saga.*** Illustrated by Leo Dillon and Diane Dillon. Houghton, 1963. — E · 6–8

This is a summary of a boy's struggles to adjust and survive the many changes that occur after the death of his father. With the support of friends, he is encouraged to regain his birthright and rule the island in an unselfish manner.

Hautzig, Esther. ***A Gift for Mama.*** Viking, 1981. — C · 5–8

Although Sara's mother has always insisted that family gifts must be handmade by the giver, Sara works to earn the money to buy beautiful satin slippers for her mother. The story is set in Poland during the 1930s.

Holling, Holling C. ***Paddle-to-the-Sea.*** Houghton, 1941. — E · 5–6

A small hand-carved canoe makes an exciting journey through the Great Lakes out into the Gulf of St. Lawrence to the sea.

Holling, Holling C. ***Tree in the Trail.*** Houghton, 1978. — E · 5–6

The tree, a 200-year-old cottonwood, stands by the Santa Fe Trail and watches as history passes by. The text is well illustrated with pencil sketches and color plates.

Levitin, Sonia. ***Journey to America.*** Atheneum, 1971. — E · 5–8

Young Lisa, with her Jewish family, escapes from the German Nazis to emigrate to America. The journey and resettlement require great courage and determination.

Lewis, Thomas P. ***Hill of Fire.*** Harper Junior Books, 1987. — C · 2–3 · H

The story, slightly fictionalized, of a real event—the eruption of a volcano in Mexico—tells of a family whose land was involved in the amazing occurrence.

Lobel, Arnold. ***On the Day Peter Stuyvesant Sailed into Town.*** Harper Junior Books, 1971. — E · 1–4

Peter Stuyvesant arrives in New Amsterdam in 1647 to rally the Dutch settlers in the effort of creating a thriving, pleasant town.

Lord, Bette B. ***In the Year of the Boar and Jackie Robinson.*** Harper Junior Books, 1984. — C · 4–6 · C

This is a delighful story of Shirley Temple Wong and her first year in America. Pathos and humor abound as the reader sees Shirley at home and at school.

	Type of entry	Grade level	Culture

MacLachlan, Patricia. *Sarah, Plain and Tall.* Harper Junior Books, 1987. — C, 4-6

When the father of Anna and Caleb advertises for a wife, he gets a reply from Sarah, who has always lived by the sea. She agrees to visit them in their home on the prairie. Will she stay? The anxious question has a satisfactory answer.

Meadowcroft, Enid. *By Secret Railway.* Crowell, 1948. — C, 4-6, B

Young Jim, a freed slave, is befriended by David, a young white boy in Chicago during the 1860s. Jim falls prey to an unscrupulous man who hopes to gain a reward for returning a runaway slave, but David rescues his friend.

Moeri, Louise. *Save Queen of Sheba.* Dutton, 1981. — E, 5-7

Two children are separated from the wagon train, and it takes all of King David's courage and energy to take care of his sister, Queen of Sheba. He manages to get them back to their parents and away from the Indians.

Monjo, F. N. *The Drinking Gourd.* Illustrated by Fred Brenner. Harper Junior Books, 1983. — C, 3-5, B

Tommy discovers that his family's farm is a stop on the Underground Railway, and his father is actually helping runaway slaves in their escape to freedom.

O'Dell, Scott. *Carlota.* Houghton, 1977. — E, 4-6

Raised to take the place of her dead brother, Carlota de Zubaran races her stallion through the California lowlands, dives into shark-infested waters, searches for gold, and fights the battles that rage between Mexico and America for possession of California.

O'Dell, Scott. *Island of the Blue Dolphins* (California). Houghton, 1960. — C, 5-6, I

This unusual story is based on the fact that in the 1800s an Indian girl spent 18 years alone on a rocky island off the coast of California.

O'Dell, Scott. *Zia.* Houghton, 1976; Dell, 1978. — E, 5-6

Zia and her brother journey to San Nicolas Island to rescue Karana, who finds it hard to adjust to mission life as she continues to long for her island life. This is a sequel to *Island of the Blue Dolphins.*

Orlev, Uri. *The Island on Bird Street.* Translated from Hebrew by Hillel Halkin. Houghton, 1984. — C, 5-6

Entirely alone in a Polish ghetto, Alex waits for his father to return for him after the Nazis imprison everyone else.

Peck, Richard. *The Ghost Belonged to Me.* Viking, 1975; Dell, 1983. — E, 5-6

A light "romp" with interesting characters results in plenty of laughs. There are enough shivery incidents to qualify this as a mystery, too.

	Type of entry	Grade level	Culture

Shub, Elizabeth. *The White Stallion.* Greenwillow, 1982; Bantam, 1982. — **C** · 3–5

While traveling west, Gretchen and her horse are separated from her family's wagon train. After many ordeals, they are rescued from a band of wild horses by a magnificent white stallion.

Speare, Elizabeth G. *The Sign of the Beaver.* Houghton, 1983; Dell, 1984. — **C** · 4–6 · I

A young boy is separated from his pioneering family in the woods of Maine. Helped by Indians, Matt gains insight into a new culture.

Speare, Elizabeth G. *The Witch of Blackbird Pond.* Houghton, 1958; Dell, 1972. — **E** · 5–7

Kit Tyler leaves Barbados to visit Puritan relatives in colonial Connecticut. There, she befriends a "witch" named Hannah. Kit is later accused of witchcraft and is brought to trial.

Sperry, Armstrong. *Call It Courage.* Macmillan, 1968, 1971. — **C** · 4–6

Mafatu, a Polynesian chieftain's son, must overcome his fear of the sea, which claimed his mother's life. His heroic journey gains him the respect of his people.

Taylor, Mildred. *Roll of Thunder, Hear My Cry.* Dial Books, 1976; Bantam, 1983. — **C** · 6–8 · B

The Logan family is unforgettable in its determination to rise above the prejudices that existed in Mississippi during the 1930s. Cassis finally understands why the land means so much to the independence of her black family.

Taylor, Sydney. *All-of-a-Kind Family.* Follett, 1951; Dell, 1966. — **E** · 4–6

The memorable childhood experiences of five sisters growing up in a Jewish family in the New York of 1912 are described.

Taylor, Theodore. *The Cay.* Doubleday, 1969; Avon, 1977. — **E** · 5–6 · B

Phillip is separated from his mother by a shipwreck, leaving him blind and marooned on a Caribbean Island. He befriends a wise West Indian sailor who helps him to survive.

Uchida, Yoshiko. *Journey Home.* Illustrated by Charles Robinson. Atheneum, 1978. — **E** · 4–6 · J

After being released from an American concentration camp, a Japanese-American girl and her family try to reconstruct their lives amidst a community's anti-Japanese feelings.

Uchida, Yoshiko. *Journey to Topaz.* Illustrated by Donald Carrick. Scribner, 1971; Creative Arts, 1985. — **C** · 4–6 · J

After the attack on Pearl Harbor, an eleven-year-old Japanese-American girl and her family are forced to go to a relocation center in Utah.

> THE EMPHASIS DURING READING LESSONS SHOULD BE ON UNDERSTANDING AND APPRECIATING THE CONTENT OF THE STORY.

	Type of entry	Grade level	Culture

Wilder, Laura I. *Little House in the Big Woods.* Illustrated by Garth Williams. Harper Junior Books, 1953, 1986.

	Type of entry	Grade level	Culture
	C	3–6	

The first of Laura's nine books describes the cabin in the big woods of Wisconsin, the daily lives of pioneers, the love of family and relatives, and the events experienced by the Ingalls family.

Wilder, Laura I. *On the Banks of Plum Creek.* Illustrated by Garth Williams. Harper Junior Books, 1965, 1986.

	Type of entry	Grade level	Culture
	E	5–6	

In the fourth book the Ingalls move to their home in Minnesota where they settle down in a dugout home. The family endures such hardships as a grasshopper plague and a blizzard. Laura goes to school and learns how to read, how to deal with people, and how to sacrifice. The family survives but at considerable cost.

NONFICTION—INFORMATION

Nonfiction, which includes both biographies and general informational material, is a crucial addition to a recommended reading list. As students proceed in school, they must spend increasing amounts of time reading for information. It is at this point that they are often "turned off" to reading, feeling that the material is dry and uninteresting. While it is important that required subject matter be covered, it is also important that the books have literary merit and present a point of view as fairly and impartially as possible.

	Type of entry	Grade level	Culture

Aliki. *Corn Is Maize: The Gift of the Indians.* Crowell, 1976.

	Type of entry	Grade level	Culture
	C	3–6	I

This story describes how corn was discovered and used by the Indians and how it came to be an important food throughout the world.

Aliki. *Digging Up Dinosaurs.* Crowell, 1981.

	Type of entry	Grade level	Culture
	E	1–3	

This book introduces various types of dinosaurs whose skeletons and reconstructions are seen in museums; and it explains how scientists uncover, preserve, and study fossilized dinosaur bones.

Aliki. *The Story of Johnny Appleseed.* Prentice-Hall, 1963.

	Type of entry	Grade level	Culture
	C	2–4	

Wandering over the land he loved, among the settlers and Indians he befriended, Johnny Appleseed planted the seeds that grew into young trees loaded with bright red apples.

	Type of entry	Grade level	Culture

Ancona, George. **Bananas: From Manolo to Margie.** Houghton, 1982. — C, 3–5

The labor of the many people who tend to bananas (farm workers, longshoremen, shippers, truckers, merchants, and more) is described. The life and work of families in Honduras is pictured.

Ancona, George. **Dancing Is.** Dutton, 1981. — E, 2–4

Black-and-white illustrations of more than 50 international dances enhance this book that can be used to introduce groups to movement.

Arnosky, Jim. **Secrets of a Wildlife Watcher.** Lothrop, 1983. — E, 3–6

Readers are encouraged to observe nature, to question, and to sharpen their skills of observation while experiencing the delight of watching animals in their natural, unguarded moments.

Baylor, Byrd. **The Desert Is Theirs** (Papago). Atheneum, n.d.; Scribner, 1975. — C, K–3, I

The author tells the reader about the desert, describing flora and fauna and respectfully paying tribute to the desert people who know its secrets and would live nowhere else.

Baylor, Byrd. **The Way to Start a Day.** Scribner, 1978. — C, 2–6

How people all over the world celebrate the sunrise is described in words and pictures.

Beatty, Patricia. **Lupita Mañana.** Morrow, 1981. — C, 5–7, H

To help her poverty-stricken family, thirteen-year-old Lupita enters California as an illegal alien and starts to work while constantly on the watch for *la migra*.

Brenner, Barbara. **On the Frontier with Mr. Audubon.** Putnam, 1977. — C, 5–8

The journal of Joseph Mason, thirteen, records his 18-month journey down the Mississippi and Ohio on a flatboat with "Mr. A," a painter who likes to paint birds.

Charlip, Remy, and Mary Beth. **Handtalk: An ABC of Finger Spelling and Sign Language.** Parents Magazine Press, 1974. — C, 2–6

This book describes two kinds of sign language: finger spelling, or forming words letter by letter with the fingers; and signing, or making signs with one or two hands for each word or idea.

De Garza, Patricia. **Chicanos: The Story of Mexican-Americans.** Messner, 1973. — C, 5–8, H

This book provides a brief overview of the 400-year history of Mexican Americans from the initial Spanish settlement in the American Southwest to modern life in the urban barrio and the migrant stream.

Demuth, Patricia. **Joel: Growing Up on Farm Man.** Dodd, 1982. — C, 6–9

Thirteen-year-old Joel Holland's life and work as a young farmer are described. Business aspects of farming, family sharing of responsibility, chores in planting and harvesting crops, and breeding and caring for animals are covered.

	Type of entry	Grade level	Culture

DePaola, Tomie. *The Quicksand Book.* Holiday, 1984. — C, 2–5

The composition of quicksand and rescue procedures are described.

Endo, Takako, and others. *Japanese-American Journey: The Story of a People.* Edited by Florence Hongo and Miyo Burton. Japanese American Curriculum Project, 1985. — E, 5–8, J

This book presents the culture and history of Japanese Americans from the 1800s to the present. Ten brief biographies and three short stories are included.

Epstein, Beryl, and Samuel Epstein. *Doctor Beaumont and the Man with the Hole in His Stomach.* Coward, 1978. — E, 3–5

Interesting experiments concerning digestion are described in this biography of a curious physician who had an unusual patient.

Freedman, Russell. *Children of the Wild West.* Houghton, 1983. — E, 5–8

Children of pioneer families travel west in a wagon train. Documentary photographs are included in this story of their experiences.

Gemming, Elizabeth. *Lost City in the Clouds: The Discovery of Machu Picchu.* Coward, 1980. — E, 5–7

The author recounts historian Bingham's discovery. The book describes both legend and fact about the Incas in the Andean region.

Gibbons, Gail. *Fire! Fire!* Crowell Junior Books, 1984. — E, 2–4

Gibbons explores different types of fires (in the city, in the country, in the forest, and on the waterfront) and the firefighters' approach to them.

Gibbons, Gail. *The Post Office Book.* Crowell Junior Books, 1982. — E, 2–5

Many types of post offices, workers, and mailboxes as well as a brief history of mail and interesting mail facts are included. This is an excellent book for a class studying community helpers.

Giblin, James C. *Chimney Sweeps.* Crowell Junior Books, 1982. — E, 4–7

The history and folklore of the chimney-sweeping profession are traced from the fifteenth century to the present day, with emphasis on the plight of the often-abused climbing boys of past centuries.

Isenbart, Hans-Heinrich. *A Duckling Is Born.* Putnam, 1981. — C, 2–4

A mallard drake and duck, with their offspring, are featured in a simple, appealing photographic essay that introduces the principles of life cycle and embryology.

Kohl, Herbert, and Judith Kohl. *The View from the Oak.* Scribner, 1977. — C, 3–5

An oak tree may be a home to a fox, a nest for a beetle, and a source of food for a woodpecker.

	Type of entry	Grade level	Culture

Krementz, Jill. *A Very Young Rider.* Knopf, 1977. `C` `3–6`

By observing an actual ten-year-old girl as she cares for her pony, learns to ride, and participates in shows, the reader learns about the responsibilities as well as pleasures of having a horse.

Kuskin, Karla. *The Philharmonic Gets Dressed.* Illustrated by Marc Simont. Harper Junior Books, 1982. `C` `2–5`

The reader learns how 105 musicians prepare for their concert.

Lasker, Joe. *Merry Ever After: The Story of Two Medieval Weddings.* Viking, 1976. `E` `3–6`

This book contrasts the plans, ceremonies, and expectations of two couples getting married in the Middle Ages. Simple text and interesting illustrations have been used.

Lasky, Kathryn. *Sugaring Time.* Macmillan, 1983. `E` `5–6`

A photographic essay depicts the hard work and pleasure of collecting maple sap and converting it into syrup for the table.

Lasky, Kathryn. *The Weaver's Gift.* Warne, 1980. `E` `5–7`

This book traces the steps from the birth of a lamb through shearing and then the processing of wool through the sorting, grading, spinning, dyeing, and weaving that are required to make a blanket for a small boy.

Lauber, Patricia. *Seeds: Pop Stick Glide.* Crown, 1981. `C` `K–3`

The journeys of different seeds are enhanced by large close-up photographs (in black and white).

Lauber, Patricia. *What's Hatching Out of That Egg?* Crown, 1979. `C` `1–3`

Presented in the form of a guessing game, the simple text and the accompanying close-up photographs show the way 11 animals are born.

Lester, Julius. *To Be a Slave.* Dial Books, 1968. `E` `6–9` `B`

The vivid account of how it felt to be a slave is based on material gathered from actual men and women who had been slaves.

Loeper, John J. *The House on Spruce Street.* Atheneum, 1982. `E` `5–9`

The author traces the story of a particular, though fictional, house in Philadelphia.

Meyers, Susan. *Pearson, a Harbor Seal Pup.* Dutton, 1981. `C` `4–8`

The staff at the California Marine Mammal Center rescues and rehabilitates an orphaned harbor seal.

Michel, Anna. *The Story of Nim: The Chimp Who Learned Language.* Random House, 1980. `E` `4–6`

This is a true story of how a chimp was trained to use sign language. Nim was raised from infancy as if he were a human baby, and at the age of four he had a vocabulary of 125 signs.

	Type of entry	Grade level	Culture

Nance, John. *Lobo of the Tasaday: A Stone Age Boy Meets the Modern World.* Pantheon, 1982. — **E** | **3–6** |

This is a story of a boy named Lobo, who was ten years old when the Tasaday were discovered in the Philippines in 1971. The book describes how Lobo and 25 others were living in a stone age culture and re-creates their first meeting with the modern world.

Pace, Mildred. *Wrapped for Eternity: The Story of the Egyptian Mummy.* McGraw-Hill, 1974. — **E** | **5–8** |

This book discusses natural and embalmed mummies from frozen mastodons to the mummies of ancient Egypt. It explains how and why mummies were made and how they have been found. The attitudes and superstitions about them are also discussed.

Patterson, Francine. *Koko's Kitten.* Scholastic, 1985. — **C** | **2–6** |

Koko, a sign-language-using gorilla, receives a kitten as a pet, loves it, and grieves its death. This true story is depicted with large color photos.

Politi, Leo. *Song of the Swallows.* Scribner, 1949. — **E** | **1–5** | **H**

A young boy named Juan and the gardener at the Mission San Juan Capistrano love the swallows that live there. Juan makes a garden for the birds at his house. After celebrating the return of the swallows at the mission, Juan comes home to find swallows nesting in his own garden.

Price, Christine. *Dancing Masks of Africa.* Scribner, 1975. — **C** | **1–4** |

Using a poetic text and dramatic block prints, the author explains the role of ceremonial masks in West African culture and describes how masks are used in rituals of supplication or celebration.

Rockwell, Anne. *The Toolbox.* Macmillan, 1971. — **C** | **3–5** |

The author of this picture book describes the contents of a toolbox and explains the uses of each tool. The brief text is printed in clear, handsome type.

Sattler, Helen Roney. *Dinosaurs of North America.* Lothrop, 1981. — **E** | **3–6** |

This is an up-to-date book on dinosaurs. The casual reader may find this book somewhat difficult to enjoy, but dinosaur buffs will thoroughly relish this gold mine of information with its interesting drawings.

Scott, Jack Denton. *The Book of the Pig.* Putnam, 1981. — **E** | **4–6** |

The author dispels fallacies about the eating and hygienic habits of pigs and describes the value of using pigs in modern scientific studies (including studies on jogging during which some pigs ran two miles a day). The book also provides a history of the species from the prehistoric tusked hog to today's domesticated pig.

Selsam, Millicent E. *Cotton.* Morrow, 1982. — **C** | **3–5** |

The author begins with a brief history of cotton and discusses the major area of the world in which it has been grown and processed. The history section ends with a description of several inventions that reduce the time necessary to process cotton. Then, the cotton plant's growth and maturation are described and shown with photos.

	Type of entry	Grade level	Culture

Selsam, Millicent E. *The Maple Tree*. Morrow, 1968.

Using the Norway maple to demonstrate the principles of growth, the author and photographer describe the step-by-step development of a seed into a tree from the winged fruit that puts roots into the ground and produces buds, leaves, and branches. This is an informative botany book for the primary grade reader.

C   2–5

Selsam, Millicent. *See Through the Forest*. Harper Junior Books, 1956.

The author describes a forest from bottom to top, comparing it to a tall building. Each "floor" has its own climate and tenants (for example, the "basement" has dead leaves, beetles, ants, mold, spongy soil, and earthworms). Bushes, birds, and other animals are introduced at different levels.

C   2–4

St. George, Judith. *The Brooklyn Bridge: They Said It Couldn't Be Built*. Putnam, 1982.

Having done research on the Roebling letters, notebooks, reports, scrapbooks, and other primary sources, the author presents a clear, detailed text with illustrations that help to convey the drama of the dangerous building process. She describes the fascinating history of the most photographed, most painted, and most written about structure in America.

C   5–9

Tunis, Edwin. *Frontier Living*. Harper Junior Books, 1976.

This book introduces white settlements in North America by area and by epoch. It describes life as it was, not as later romanticized. It includes details and illustrations on such items as cabins, food, clothes, and inns.

E   4–7

Weaver, Harriett E. *Frosty: A Raccoon to Remember*. Chronicle Books, 1973.

This book describes the humorous, scary, and heartwarming adventures of Frosty, a raccoon raised by the author when she was a ranger at Big Basin Redwood Park. The book has good black-and-white line drawings.

E   5–6

Wolf, Bernard. *Don't Feel Sorry for Paul*. Lippincott, 1974.

Written in the form of a documentary, this book presents the highlights of several weeks in the life of Paul Jockimo, a child born without a right hand and foot and with a deformed left hand and foot. In stark pictures with accompanying text, we see Paul's deformities and watch as he puts on the three prosthetic devices. We follow him bicycling, playing, going to school, celebrating his seventh birthday, and finally, winning second prize in a horse show.

E   5–8

Yue, Charlotte. *The Tipi: A Center of Native American Life*. Knopf, 1983.

In addition to describing the structure, uses, and furnishings of domestic and ceremonial tipis, the author gives a great deal of information about the cultural patterns of the various peoples known as the Great Plains Indians. The black-and-white drawings are meticulously detailed.

E   5–6   I

NONFICTION – BIOGRAPHY

Biography presents a special challenge to students. Through reading about the lives of others, who may have overcome great adversities or handicaps, students may begin to realize the opportunities and situations that they may confront. They may also find solutions to perplexing personal questions or situations. It is for these reasons that nonfiction titles for students should be selected as carefully as those in other categories are selected.

	Type of entry	Grade level	Culture
Adoff, Arnold. *Malcolm X.* Harper Junior Books, 1972. This short biography vividly outlines the events, both tragic and rewarding, that influenced the life and thought of Malcolm X from childhood to death and clearly shows his significance as a black leader.	E	6–8	B
Aliki. *The Many Lives of Benjamin Franklin.* Prentice-Hall, 1977. This is a picture book story of Benjamin Franklin's life. It touches on his inventiveness, and it describes his careers as writer, printer, politician, and diplomat.	E	1–3	
Aliki. *A Weed Is a Flower: The Life of George Washington Carver.* Prentice-Hall, 1965. This is a read-aloud picture book biography that gives a fairly balanced picture of Dr. Carver as a person and of his work as a researcher and teacher.	C	2–4	B
Barnard, Jacqueline. *Voices from the Southwest: Antonio José Martinez, Elfego Baca, and Reies Lopez Tijerina.* Scholastic, 1972. The author describes the struggles of three Mexican Americans in various historical periods to redress the wrongs that their people suffered.	C	4–6	H
Bertol, Roland. *Charles Drew.* Crowell, 1970. The author presents a fictionalized biography of the black doctor who discovered how to make blood transfusions and how to preserve blood.	E	4–6	B
Clayton, Edward. *Martin Luther King: The Peaceful Warrior.* Prentice-Hall, 1968. This is a biography of the black leader who tried to achieve equality for his race through nonviolent methods.	E	4–6	B

	Type of entry	Grade level	Culture

D'Aulaire, Ingri, and Edgar P. D'Aulaire. ***Columbus.*** Double-day, 1955. — E — 3–6

The authors give an account of Columbus's four voyages to the New World. The story has the excitement of exploring the unknown, and the full-page illustrations give a feeling of the times.

Faber, Doris. ***Eleanor Roosevelt: First Lady of the World.*** Viking, 1985. — E — 3–6

Eleanor Roosevelt had enormous political influence and won love and respect as America's first lady. In this biography the author emphasizes Mrs. Roosevelt's early years.

Faber, Doris. ***Oh, Lizzie! The Life of Elizabeth Cady Stanton.*** Lothrop, 1972. — E — 5–7

Elizabeth Cady Stanton carried the crusade for women's rights from Maine to California.

Fall, Thomas. ***Jim Thorpe.*** Crowell, 1970. — E — 3–5 — I

This biography examines the abilities of Jim Thorpe, one of the world's finest all-around athletes. It tells how out of his early experiences came the skills which later made him famous.

Feinberg, Barbara S. ***Franklin D. Roosevelt, Gallant President.*** Lothrop, 1981. — E — 5–6

The author describes Franklin D. Roosevelt, who served as president for more than 12 years, longer than any other president.

Fox, Mary V. ***Jane Goodall: Living Chimp Style.*** Dillon Press, 1981. — E — 3–5

This is a biography of the first scientist to study chimpanzees in their natural habitat.

Franchere, Ruth. ***Cesar Chavez.*** Crowell, 1970. — C — 4–8 — H

This is a biography of Cesar Chavez, who organized the grape pickers of California and led a nationwide grape boycott to get better wages and working conditions for migrant workers.

Fritz, Jean. ***And Then What Happened, Paul Revere?*** Illustrated by Margot Tomes. Coward, 1973. — C — 3–6

This description of Paul Revere's ride to Lexington is funny, fast-paced, and historically accurate.

Fritz, Jean. ***Homesick: My Own Story.*** Putnam, 1982. — E — 5–6

The author gives a fictionalized version, though all the events are true, of her childhood in China in the 1920s and 1930s.

Fritz, Jean. ***What's the Big Idea, Ben Franklin?*** Illustrated by Margot Tomes. Coward, 1976. — C — 3–6

This well-researched and documented biography reflects the humor, virtues, flaws, and zest for living characteristic of the subject.

	Type of entry	Grade level	Culture
Fritz, Jean. ***Where Was Patrick Henry on the 29th of May?*** Coward, 1975.	C	3–6	
Using the date of Patrick Henry's birth, May 29, the author focuses on significant periods in the patriot's life.			
Fritz, Jean. ***Why Don't You Get a Horse, Sam Adams?*** Coward, 1974.	E	3–5	
Samuel Adams refuses to ride a horse while agitating in Boston against British rule.			
Greenfeld, Howard. ***Marc Chagall: An Introduction.*** Overlook Press, 1980.	C	5–7	
This biography of the Russian-born artist includes illustrations of his work.			
Hautzig, Esther. ***Endless Steppe: A Girl in Exile.*** Crowell, 1968.	E	6–9	
This is a true story of a child and her family's five difficult years in Siberia during their exile from Poland.			
Hunter, Edith Fisher. ***Child of the Silent Night: The Story of Laura Bridgman.*** Houghton, 1963.	C	5–6	
The author tells about a blind and deaf girl who learns to communicate with help from her strong teacher and friend.			
Hyman, Trina S. ***Self-Portrait.*** Harper Junior Books, 1981.	E	5–6	
The author discusses her life and her art in this interesting autobiography for children.			
Jackson, Jesse. ***Make a Joyful Noise Unto the Lord: The Life of Mahalia Jackson, Queen of Gospel Singers.*** Crowell, 1974.	C	6–8	B
This is a biography of Mahalia Jackson, who tried to break down racial barriers between black and white people.			
Kohn, Bernice. ***Talking Leaves: The Story of Sequoyah.*** Hawthorn, 1969.	C	4–7	I
This is a story of a scholarly Cherokee Indian who devised a way to record the language of his people.			
Kroeber, Theodora. ***Ishi, Last of His Tribe*** (Yahi, California). Houghton, 1964.	C	5–7	I
This is a story of Ishi, the single survivor of his tribe. The book provides insights into the American Indian culture.			
Lindstrom, Aletha J. ***Sojourner Truth: Slave, Abolitionist, Fighter for Women's Rights.*** Julian Messner, 1980.	E	6–8	B
This is a biography of a former slave who became one of the best known abolitionists of her day. She spent her life trying to improve living conditions for her people.			
McCunn, Ruthanne L. ***Thousand Pieces of Gold: A Biographical Novel.*** Design Enterprises of San Francisco, 1981.	C	5–8	C
This biographical novel of Lalu Nathoy, later known as Polly Bemis, is the story of a Chinese woman and her acts of kindness.			

USE METHODS FOR INTRODUCING CHILDREN TO READINGS THAT HAVE MEANING.

	Type of entry	Grade level	Culture

McGovern, Ann. *The Secret Soldier: The Story of Deborah Sampson.* Four Winds, 1975. — C — 6–8

This is the story of an American patriot during Revolutionary War times. She travels alone, sharing her experiences through speeches about the hardships of life.

Meltzer, Milton. *Dorothea Lange: A Photographer's Life.* Farrar, 1978. — C — 4–6

This is the story of a famous twentieth-century woman photographer who brought about social reforms by her depiction of rural poverty and conditions of migrant workers' lives.

Monjo, Ferdinand N. *Letters to Horseface: Being the Story of Wolfgang Amadeus Mozart's Journey to Italy, 1769-70, When He Was a Boy of Fourteen.* Viking, 1975. — E — 5–6

This historical novel of Mozart's childhood explores the eighteenth-century world of music.

Monjo, Ferdinand N. *Me and Willie and Pa.* Simon and Schuster, 1973. — C — 4–6

This story recalls some of the great moments of Abraham Lincoln's presidency as seen through the eyes of his son Todd.

Monjo, Ferdinand N. *The One Bad Thing About Father.* Harper Junior Books, 1987. — C — 4–6

This is an invented diary of Quentin, the son of Theodore Roosevelt. The author captures the personality of the president.

Morrison, Dorothy N. *Under a Strong Wind: The Adventures of Jessie Benton Fremont.* Macmillan, 1983. — E — 6–8

This story describes the adventurous life of a daughter of a United States senator. Her husband was a frontier explorer.

Morrow, Honore W. *On to Oregon.* Morrow, 1926. — E — 4–8

The author describes the bravery of orphaned children who endure hardships and dangers on the long trek to Oregon in a covered wagon.

Newlon, Clarke. *Famous Mexican Americans.* Dodd, 1972. — E — 5–8 — H

This is a collection of biographies of 20 well-known Mexican Americans.

Nhuong, Huynh Quang. *Land I Lost.* Harper, 1982. — C — 4–7 — V

A soldier recalls time and experiences in the central highlands of Vietnam.

Provensen, Alice, and Martin Provensen. *The Glorious Flight Across the Channel with Louis Bleriot.* Viking, 1983. — C — 2–4

Louis Bleriot's fascination with flying machines led to the design of a plane that crossed the English Channel in 37 minutes in the 1900s.

Quackenbush, Robert. *Mark Twain? What Kind of a Name Is That?* Prentice-Hall, 1984. — E — 4–6

This lighthearted biography of Samuel Langhorne Clemens is for young readers.

	Type of entry	Grade level	Culture

Raboff, Ernest. *Pablo Picasso.* Doubleday, 1968.

    This small picture book, one of a series on artists, presents bits of biography and the artist's work.

| E | 5-7 | |

Reiss, Johanna. *The Journey Back.* Crowell, 1976.

    Annie of *The Upstairs Room* goes back to Holland to find the tragic aftermath of war and occupation.

| E | 5-6 | |

Reiss, Johanna. *The Upstairs Room.* Crowell, 1972.

    Annie, a European Jew, lives hidden away in a farmhouse in wartime Holland, protected by a family that put itself at great risk for her.

| C | 6-9 | |

Roberts, Naurice. *Barbara Jordan: The Great Lady from Texas.* Children's Press, 1984.

    This black woman of great courage has served both in local and state government as well as in Congress. She now is a professor in her native state.

| E | 5-7 | B |

Rockwell, Anne. *Paintbrush and Peacepipe: The Story of George Catlin.* Atheneum, 1971.

    The author tells the exciting and tragic story of this nineteenth-century North American whose paintings and writings have contributed much to our knowledge about the Plains Indians of that time.

| E | 5-6 | |

Rudeen, Kenneth. *Roberto Clemente.* Harper Junior Books, 1974.

    This is a simply written baseball story about the pride of the Pirates.

| E | 3-5 | H |

Sobol, Rose. *Woman Chief.* Dial, 1976.

    This is a fictionalized biography of a Crow Indian woman who became a leader of her people.

| E | 7-8 | I |

Syme, Ronald. *Magellan: First Around the World.* Morrow, 1953.

    This concise, clearly written biography is by the author of a long list of books about explorers.

| E | 4-6 | |

Tobias, Tobi. *Isamu Noguchi: The Life of a Sculptor.* Crowell, 1974.

    The author's interest in art is reflected in this balanced biography of a modern-day sculptor.

| C | 3-6 | J |

Tobias, Tobi. *Maria Tallchief* (Osage). Crowell, 1970.

    The author shows a lifelong interest in dance and writes with clarity of this famous American Indian ballerina.

| E | 5-7 | I |

Yates, Elizabeth. *Amos Fortune, Free Man.* Illustrated by Noras Unwin. Dutton, 1967.

    With his eyes on his future freedom from slavery, the hero endures hardships as a northern slave before winning his freedom to devote his life to buying freedom for other slaves.

| E | 6-8 | B |

Zemach, Margot. *Self-Portrait.* Addison-Wesley, 1978.

    The writer's illustrations of her life as an artist make this a doubly interesting autobiography.

| E | 5-6 | |

Plays (Kindergarten through Grade Six)

Plays are excellent for helping students to develop skills in an integrated way and at the same time to encounter some of the great enduring tales. Many of the plays listed below are adaptations from folk and fairy tales and from other literary forms, while others are plays written for special occasions. The plays can be used as puppet shows, readers' theater presentations, and full dramatizations. The titles listed here may be found in almost any public library.

Single Plays

Andersen, Hans Christian. *The Red Shoes.* Samuel French, 1986.

A magic pair of shoes causes the wearer to dance incessantly. Snogg, a gypsy, has the shoes and entices a poor Danish orphan girl, Karen, to wear them. She ends up in Snogg's traveling show where she is later rescued by Jimmo, the sad, silent clown.

Behrens, June. *Feast of Thanksgiving.* Children's Press, 1974.

A Pilgrim family prepares a Thanksgiving feast and shares it with the Indians.

Childress, Alice. *When the Rattlesnake Sounds: A Play About Harriet Tubman.* Coward, 1975.

This play is based on one summer in the life of Harriet Tubman when she worked as a laundress to raise money for the abolitionist movement.

Chorpenning, Charlotte B. *Alice in Wonderland.* Coach House, 1959.

The audience sees Alice in an enormous armchair. From there, she attends a wise but nonsensical quorum of mythical birds, discusses life with a caterpillar, and meets the Duchess, whose baby turns into a pig. Part II has Alice enter the land of the Chess Queens, where time and space are defied.

Chorpenning, Charlotte B. *Hansel and Gretel.* Coach House, 1956.

With a bare cupboard, a stepmother leaves little Hansel and Gretel deep in the forest to fend for themselves. Their playmates try to find them but are captured by Wicked Witch. Hansel and Gretel are also caught but escape and outwit their captor. The stepmother regrets her actions, and all go home to live happily.

Chorpenning, Charlotte B. *Rip Van Winkle.* Coach House, 1954 (Children's Theatre Playscript Series).

This play is based on one of America's best-known and best-loved folklore characters, Rip Van Winkle, who, on one of his jaunts, falls asleep for 20 years.

Davis, Ossie. *Escape to Freedom: A Play About Young Frederick Douglass.* Viking, 1978.

The author presents episodes from the life of Frederick Douglass: his childhood in a slave cabin, his zeal in learning how to read, his treatment on a slave-breaking plantation, his experiences in Baltimore, and his escape to New York.

Evernden, Margery. *King Author's Sword.* Coach House, 1959.

This play is based on one of the many legends about King Arthur, the hero of many stories of the Middle Ages.

Evernden, Margery. *Rumpelstiltskin.* Coach House, 1955.

This children's play is based on the original fairy tale of *Rumpelstiltskin.*

Fox, Phyllis, and David Coleman. *Cinderella.* Coach House, 1978.

Although the characters in this play are from the original *Cinderella,* they are given motivation for their actions. Because of this three-dimensional quality of the characters, magic is not sufficient to solve Cinderella's problems, and her fairy godmother must enlist the aid of the White Rabbit from *Alice in Wonderland.*

Freeman, Ethel. *Heidi.*

Heidi, the little Swiss girl, loves the mountaintop home she shares with her grandfather and is miserably homesick when her aunt sends her to a far-off city in Germany, where she becomes the companion of Clara, an invalid.

Glennon, William. *Ali Baba and the Magic Cave.* Coach House, 1969.

This drama is based on the Arabian Nights tale of a woodcutter who becomes rich as the result of secret information.

Glennon, William. *Jack and the Beanstalk.* Coach House, 1969.

Jack, the spoiled son of a widow, returns from the market with magic beans instead of money. In despair, his mother flings them to the wind and they grow into a gigantic beanstalk that leads Jack to a giant and to great adventure and wealth.

Hale, Pat. *The Adventures of Brer Rabbit.*

Brer Rabbit is the trickster-hero of many of the *Uncle Remus* stories.

Hale, Pat. *The Ballad of Robin Hood.*

This play is based on the story of the legendary outlaw who robbed the rich and gave to the poor.

Hale, Pat. *The Bremen Town Musicians.*

Some aging animals, wishing to escape being put to death by their owners, set out on the road to Bremen with the intention of finding work as musicians. On their journey they discover a band of robbers whom they scare away, believing them to be ghosts.

Holloway, Dorothy. *The Steadfast Tin Soldier.*

A toy tin soldier with only one leg falls in love with a ballerina who perches delicately on one leg. After a series of disasters, their love ends as they both are blown into the fire where they perish.

Jonson, Marian. *Snow White and the Seven Dwarfs.* Coach House, 1957.

Snow White is envied by her cruel stepmother, whose magic mirror tells her that Snow White is even fairer than herself. In a rage the queen orders that Snow White shall be abandoned in a forest. Despite the evil queen's attempts against her life, Snow White survives, reaffirming that good does indeed triumph over evil.

Kraus, Joanna Halpert. *Meant to Be Free.*

This is the dramatized story of the northern flight of escapees via the Underground Railway.

Latshaw, George. *Pinocchio.* Coach House, 1959.

After Gepetto carves a table leg into the puppet, Pinocchio, he finds that it can walk and talk just as a real boy can. In fact, Pinocchio is a scamp with terrible behavior. He has an immense nose of ridiculous proportions that grows even longer when he tells a lie.

Schlesinger, Sarah. *Tom Sawyer.*

Tom, who lives with his brother Sid and Aunt Polly in a village on the Mississippi, is constantly playing truant from home and school with his friends Joe Harper and Huckleberry Finn. Their adventures make for exciting reading.

Stuart, Ellen. *Beauty and the Beast.*

Beauty, the youngest daughter of a merchant, is sent to live with the Beast to compensate for a wrongdoing by her father. Although she grows to love Beast, Beauty leaves him to visit her family, only to find him dead on her return. Her tears not only revive him but also restore his true identity, that of a handsome prince.

Anthologies and Collections of Plays

Alexander, Sue. *Small Plays for Special Days.* Houghton, 1977.

This book contains seven short plays for two actors about special holidays. Staging notes and costume suggestions are included.

Bennett, Rowena. *Creative Plays and Programs for Holidays.* Plays, Inc., 1966.

This book includes plays, playlets, group readings, poems, and seasonal programs for boys and girls.

Boiko, Claire. *Children's Plays for Creative Actors.* Plays, Inc., 1981.

This is a collection of royalty-free plays for boys and girls. Most of the plays, 35 in all, have a playing time of 15 to 30 minutes. Several are appropriate for holidays.

Cheatham, Val R. *Skits and Spoofs for Young Actors.* Plays, Inc., 1977.

This collection of one-act royalty-free plays, skits, and spoofs is for the amateur stage. Production notes are included.

Children's Plays from Favorite Stories. Edited by Sylvia Kamerman. Plays, Inc., 1970.

Fifty royalty-free plays for children in lower and middle grades are based on folktales and fairy tales such as *Snow White and the Seven Dwarfs* and *Rapunzel.*

Dramatized Folk Tales of the World. Edited by Sylvia Kamerman. Plays, Inc., 1971.

These 50 royalty-free one-act dramatizations are based on traditional folklore from 26 countries. They are easy to stage and ideal for classroom or assembly programs.

Fifty Plays for Junior Actors. Edited by Sylvia Kamerman. Plays, Inc., 1966.

These comedies, fairy tales, mysteries, and science fiction dramatizations for special occasions are entertaining plays for middle and upper grades.

Fisher, Aileen. *Holiday Programs for Boys and Girls.* Plays, Inc., 1970.

This collection includes easily produced, nonroyalty plays, poems for choral readings, group presentations, and recitations for a variety of special occasions often observed in schools.

Henderson, Nancy. *Celebrate America: A Baker's Dozen of Plays.* Simon and Schuster, 1978.

This book celebrates America throughout the whole year: a play for each month, with one to spare. Celebrations for events range from the humorous to the solemn.

Korty, Carole. *Plays from African Folktales: With Ideas for Acting, Dance, Costumes, and Music.* Scribner, 1969.

The four plays in this collection are based on a number of African tales and include the antics of Ananse and Mr. Hare. Good suggestions are included for use with these ideas and other dramatic material.

Korty, Carole. *Silly Soup: Ten Zany Plays.* Scribner, 1977.

These short, nonsensical plays are complete with songs and information about beginning theater. They can be used to introduce children to performing comic scenes with zest and delight.

Little Plays for Little Players. Edited by Sylvia Kamerman. Plays, Inc., 1952.
>These one-act plays are suitable for younger children. The subject matter should excite the child's imagination.

Mahlmann, Lewis, and David Jones. ***Puppet Plays from Favorite Stories.*** Plays, Inc., 1977.
>This book contains 18 plays from a variety of favorite stories that involve using hand and rod puppets and marionettes.

Miller, Helen L. ***First Plays for Children.*** Plays, Inc., 1960.
>This collection of short plays is designed to provide easy material for young age groups. The plays are selected for gaiety and liveliness to appeal to the interest of beginning players.

Miller, Helen L. ***Short Plays for Children.*** Plays, Inc., 1969.
>These 24 one-act royalty-free plays have themes varying from fairy tales and nursery rhyme spoofs to mysteries.

Newman, Deborah. ***Holiday Plays for Little Players.*** Plays, Inc., 1957.
>These 33 short royalty-free plays have been selected for 20 special occasions.

One Hundred Plays for Children. Edited by A. S. Burack. Plays, Inc., 1970.
>This anthology contains one-act nonroyalty plays that are suitable for the intermediate grades.

Patriotic and Historical Plays for Young People. Edited by Sylvia Kamerman. Plays, Inc., 1975.
>This collection of royalty-free plays and programs may be used to dramatize our nation's heritage.

Preston, Carol. ***A Trilogy of Christmas Plays for Children.*** Harcourt, 1967.
>These three plays for Christmas have been developed over the years by the staff of the Potomac School in Virginia. These serious, reverent dramas are simple enough for school performance.

Rockwell, Thomas. ***How to Eat Fried Worms.*** Delacorte, 1980.
>This book of four plays includes the adaptation of Rockwell's popular 1973 novel about two boys who set out to prove that worms can make a delicious meal. Productions and props are fairly simple.

Thane, Adele. ***Plays from Famous Stories and Fairy Tales.*** Plays, Inc., 1967.
>This collection of 28 plays is based on stories of Western European and American origin, ranging from fairy tales to Tom Sawyer. Production notes are given for each play.

Treasury of Christmas Plays. Edited by Sylvia Kamerman. Plays, Inc., 1975.
>These 40 one-act plays for young people reveal the true spirit of Christmas. They include contemporary comedies, dramatizations of the Christmas story, and serious dramas.

BOOKS IN LANGUAGES OTHER THAN ENGLISH

Books that are written in languages other than English are suggested for children who read in another language better than they can in English. The books are acknowledged literature of merit and take their place alongside the English language books. These books are listed to ensure that the children who use another language have the same opportunity to read and enjoy the benefits of literature until they can read in English.

This category could include books from many languages; however, several factors mitigate against listing them all. Therefore, we have limited our entries to those in Chinese, Japanese, Korean, Spanish, and Vietnamese. Although California now has many Pacific Island Americans, the compilers of this document have searched without success for published literature suitable to the children of this group. It is hoped that their folk literature and stories soon can be published for use in the schools. Books that are translated into several languages, such as *Snow White and the Seven Dwarfs,* are included in both the English and other language lists.

The matrix to the right of each listing gives the user the following information:

1. Designation of core (C) or recreational/motivational (R) material
2. The suggested grade span
3. The language in which the book is written;

C — Chinese	S — Spanish
J — Japanese	V — Vietnamese
K — Korean	

Picture Books

	Type of entry	Grade level	Language
Alcantara Sgarb, Ricardo. **Guaragu.** Illustrated by Maria Rius. Barcelona: Editorial La Galera, 1978.	R	4–6	S
Guaragu, a young Indian boy, finds a beautiful bluebird by the edge of the forest and seeks to befriend it. Both the illustrations and text convey a sympathetic picture of life in a culture that remains close to nature.			
Armijo, Consuelo. **Mone.** Illustrated by Montse Ginesta. Valladolid: Miñon, 1981.	R	K–3	S
The story of a little girl and her teddy bear, Mone, is beautifully illustrated.			
Ballesta, Juan. **Tommy y el elefante.** Editorial Lumen, 1983.	R	K–3	S
Tommy, a red-headed British boy, has an imaginary and invisible elephant named Pac. The humorous story is illustrated in color.			

	Type of entry	Grade level	Language

Baum, Willi. *La expedición.* Caracas: Ediciones Ekare-Banco del Libro, 1977. — R · K–3 · S

In this humorous story—told entirely in pictures—a captain discovers an island and decides to conquer it. There is quite a surprise awaiting him when he and his sailors, with all the loot, return to the ship.

Broger, Achim, and Gisela Kalow. *Buenos días, querida Ballena.* Barcelona: Editorial Juventud, 1978. — R · K–3 · S

Enrique, the fisherman, goes out to sea where he meets Ballena, the whale, beginning a long and warm friendship.

Burningham, John. *Trubloff, el ratón que quería tocar la balalaika.* — R · 4–6 · S

A mouse that runs away with gypsies to learn to play the balalaika returns home just in time to save his family.

Claret, Maria. *La ratita Blasa.* — R · K–3 · S

Blasa is looking for a mate. This theme is used to lead the reader through the months of the year. Each season is introduced by old-fashioned drawings. Blasa finally meets Ratón Gris.

Coutant, Helen. *First Snow.* Knopf, 1974. — C · 1–3 · C

With the help of her grandmother and the first snow she has ever seen, a little Vietnamese girl begins to understand how death can be accepted as a natural part of the life cycle.

Ginester-Maestres. *El sombrero de Juan.* Barcelona: Editorial Juventud, 1977. — R · K–3 · S

Although Juan is unaware of its powers, his magic hat produces all kinds of beautiful things. It takes a strong wind to blow the hat away and allow Juan to enjoy what surrounds him.

Hazen, Nancy. *Los adultos también lloran (Grownups Cry Too).* Lollipop Power, 1984. — C · 1–3 · S

A little boy discovers that everybody cries sometimes.

Krahn, Fernando. *Hilderita y Maximiliano.* Translated by Marta Ferres. — R · K–3 · S

This delightful picture book depicts the friendship, courtship, and marriage of two ladybugs. The text is brief and printed in easy-to-read type for beginning readers. The illustrations are colorful and attractive.

Leaf, Munro. *El cuento de Ferdinando* (Spanish translation). Scholastic, 1962. — C · K–3 · S

A playful bull refuses to fight in the big Spanish bullfight. He would rather sit and smell the flowers.

Lionni, Leo. *Nadarín* (English title *Swimmy*). Translated by Ana Maria Matute. — R · K–3 · S

A little black fish discovers a safe way to show a school of little red fish the marvels of the ocean by swimming together to form the shape of a larger fish. This story helps children discover strength within themselves to surpass difficulties.

	Type of entry	Grade level	Language
Lobel, Arnold. *Mouse Tales.* Harper Junior Books, 1972.	R	K–3	S
Papa Mouse tells a "mouse tale" to each of the mouse children to help them fall asleep.			
Loof, Jan. *Mi abuelo es pirata.*	R	K–3	S
Grandfather likes to tell stories of his days as a pirate, while grandmother claims them all to be untrue; he was a postmaster all his life. One afternoon while the grandmother is taking a nap, the grandfather puts on his pirate suit and takes his grandson on a series of humorous adventures.			
Marzot, Janet, and Livio Marzot. *Las liebres blancas.*	R	K–3	S
The tracks of invisible hares in a snowy forest lead a discouraged artist to take up his pencil and brush again. The artwork is delicate pencil and brushwork in monochrome black or brown on the white snow.			
Perrault, Charles. *La cenicienta* (English title *Cinderella*). Translated by José Emilio Pacheco. Promociones Editoriales Mexicanas, 1982.	R	4–6	S
A mistreated stepdaughter, with the help of her fairy godmother, attends the palace ball. At midnight she has to leave, losing her glass slipper, which allows the prince to find her.			
Proysen, Alf. *Señora Cucharita Story Collection.* Iaconi, n.d.	R	K–3	S
Each chapter is a story in itself.			
Turin, Adela, and Nella Bosnia. *Arturo y Clementina.* Barcelona: Editorial Lumen, n.d.	R	K–3	S
This beautifully illustrated book is about two turtles, Arturo and Clementina. Arturo considers it his duty to provide for Clementina, and he piles loads of objects on her until she can hardly move. Clementina's wish is not to possess beautiful things made by others but to try her own abilities.			
Turin, Adela, and Nella Bosnia. *Una feliz catástrofe.* Barcelona: Editorial Lumen, 1976.	R	4–6	S
Life moves in an orderly fashion in the home of Mr. and Mrs. Mouse. He goes to his office; she keeps house; and the children listen to stories of the adventures of their father. An unexpected catastrophe changes everyone's life, and Mrs. Mouse's abilities are discovered.			
Tusquets, Esther. *La conejita Marcela.*	R	4–6	S
This is a contemporary animal fable about racial segregation. A white rabbit and a black rabbit start a colony of their own offspring, who are shades of gray and equal in status. This moral tale is illustrated effectively in black and white.			

CHILDREN OF EVERY
AGE AND ABILITY OUGHT
TO BE DOING MORE
EXTENDED SILENT
READING.

Folklore

	Type of entry	Grade level	Language

Ada, Alma Flor, and Maria del Pilar de Olave. *A serrín, aserrán.*
Donars Productions, Loveland (Colorado), 1979.
— C, K–3, S

This short collection contains carefully selected rhymes, riddles, games, and lullabies.

Bayley, Nicola. *Canciones tontas* (Spanish version by Javier Roca). Barcelona: Editorial Lumen, 1982.
— R, K–3, S

The rhymes of Mother Goose are presented.

Bravo-Villansante, Carmen. *Adivina, adivinanza.* Madrid: Interduc/Schroedel, 1978.
— R, K–3, S

This book includes riddles, tongue twisters, games, songs, brief stories, tall tales, lullabies, Christmas carols, and prayers.

Caballero, Fernán. *El pájaro de la verdad y otros cuentos.*
Barcelona: Editorial Labor, 1970.
— C, 4–6, S

This collection of folktales and legends includes many humorous stories.

Ching, Annie. *Birthday Party (and Other Tales).* Asian American Bilingual Center, 1978.
— C, K–6, C

A five-year-old Filipino girl is disappointed, because she is unable to get a better birthday gift from her father.

Grimm, Jacob, and Wilhelm Grimm (Spanish version by Felipe Garrido). ***Blanca Nieves y los siete enanos.*** Illustrated by Nancy E. Burkert. Farrar, 1972.
— C, 4–6, S

This is a visually spectacular Spanish version of the old tale of *Snow White and the Seven Dwarfs*. Nancy Burkert's big, framed, imaginative illustrations make the picture book lovely to look at.

Hap, Le Huy. *Vietnamese Legends.* Tuttle, 1965.
— R, 3–8, V

Traditional tales from Indo-China have been adapted by a former director of the Vietnamese-American Association.

Jimenez, Emma, and Conchita Puncel. *Para chiquitines.*
Illustrated by Gilbert T. Martinez. Bowmar, 1969.
— R, K–3, S

In this collection of songs, rhymes, and finger plays, musical notations are provided for the songs. Explanations and translations of the finger plays are also included.

Menotti, G. C. *Amahl y los Reyes Magos.* Barcelona: Editorial Lumen, 1963.
— C, 7–8, S

In this Christmas tale a young crippled boy joins the Wise Men in their journey to Jerusalem. Because he has no other gift, he offers his most valued possession, his crutch, and afterwards discovers that he needs it no longer.

Nguyen, Lan. *Vietnamese Folktales.* Office of the Alameda County Superintendent of Schools, 1981.
— R, 3–8, V

This is a good collection of familiar Vietnamese folktales.

Pushkin, Alexander. *El cuento del gallo de oro.* Illustrated by E. Bilibin. Crowell, 1975.
— C, K–3, S

This is a beautifully illustrated Spanish version of Pushkin's retelling of the Russian folktale. The golden cockerel crows and points in warning whenever the kingdom of Czar Dadon is invaded.

	Type of entry	Grade level	Language

Rohmer, Harriet. *The Legend of Food Mountain: La montaña del alimento.* Children's Books, 1982.

| | R | 4–6 | S |

Written in English and Spanish, this is a retelling of an Aztec legend based on the Chimalpopocatl codex. The god Quetzalcoatl creates man but has nothing to feed him. A giant red ant appears and shows him the way to Food Mountain.

Schultz de Mantovani, Fryda. *Leyendas argentinas.* Madrid: Editorial Aguilar, 1968.

| | R | 7–8 | S |

This is a nicely illustrated collection of Argentinian legends, myths, and stories.

Singer, Isaac Bashevis. *Cuentos judíos de la aldea de Chelm* (English title *Zlateh the Goat and Other Stories*). Illustrated by Maurice Sendak. Barcelona: Editorial Lumen, 1979.

| | R | 4–6 | S |

This book contains seven short folk stories of the Jewish town of Chelm in Poland. The small volume is beautifully illustrated. The author is a Nobel Prize winner.

Thong, Le Tinh. *Popular Stories from Vietnam* (Volume 1). Institute for Cultural Pluralism, School of Education, San Diego State University, 1977.

| | R | 4–8 | V |

This edition has been adapted in simple English by Vietnamese teachers studying at the English Language Institute, Victoria University, Wellington, New Zealand.

Two Brothers and Their Magic Gourds. Edited by Edward B. Adams. Tuttle, 1981.

| | C | 2–8 | K |

This is part of a series of Korean folk stories for children.

Wyndham, Robert. *Chinese Mother Goose Rhymes.* Philomel, 1968.

| | C | K–2 | C |

This is a beautifully illustrated edition of traditional Chinese rhymes, riddles, and games. It is designed to be read vertically as in an oriental scroll, with the original Chinese version of the verses, in correct calligraphy, flowing lengthwise on the pages.

Modern Fantasy

Andersen, Hans Christian. *Almendrita* (English title *Thumbelina).* Illustrated by Susan Jeffers. Promociones Editoriales Mexicanas, 1982.

| | C | 4–6 | S |

This is a nice version of the original story.

Balzola, Ana. *El camisón bordado.* Illustrated by Asún Balzola. Valladolid: Editorial Miñon, 1982.

| | R | K–3 | S |

In this modern fairy tale, a little girl is helped with her tasks by the fairies.

Han, Mieko. *The Marriage of a Mouse.* Institute for Intercultural Studies, Los Angeles, n.d.

| | R | 1–3 | J |

This is a traditional folktale of Father Mouse's search for the "greatest" marriage partner for his daughter. The Sun, the Cloud, the Wind, and the Wall each try to claim the title of "greatest." Finally, the perfect partner is found—a mouse that is strong enough to put a hole in the Wall. The story ends with a traditional wedding ceremony.

	Type of entry	Grade level	Language

Han, Mieko. *Turtle Power—Vietnamese.* National Asian Center for Bilingual Education, 1983. — C / 1–6 / V

Every page of this Vietnamese folktale is in English and Vietnamese. A turtle saves the life of the Dragon King, who lives in the sea, by going ashore and bringing back ginseng to heal the king.

Martí, José. *La edad de oro.* Editorial Letras Cubanas, 1979. — R / 4–6 / S

This is a facsimile of the four issues of the children's magazine by the same name.

Roxlo, Conrado Nale. *La escuela de las hadas.* Illustrated by Leonardo Haleblian. Editorial Universitaria de Buenos Aires, 1963. — R / K–3 / S

In this fantasy a young girl is a student at a school for fairies, where Merlin is the teacher, and a magical painted clown on the ceiling serves as the recess bell.

Wilde, Oscar. *El príncipe feliz.* Illustrated by Joanna Isles. Promociones Editoriales Mexicanas (distributed by Iaconi), 1982. — R / 4–6 / S

The generous statue of a prince gives all he has for those who suffer, and a swallow sacrifices her own life while acting as the prince's messenger.

Poetry

Ferran, Jaime. *Tarde del circo.* Illustrated by Carlos D'Ors. Valladolid: Miñon, 1982. — R / 4–6 / S

Young children should enjoy these poems.

Freyre de Matos, Isabel. *ABC de Puerto Rico.* Illustrated by Antonio Martorell. Sharon Troutman, Connecticut, 1968. — R / K–3 / S

Poems accompany each letter in this well-illustrated collection.

Fuertes, Gloria. *Aurora, Brigida y Carlos.* Illustrated by Jan Pienkowski. Editorial Lumen (distributed by Iaconi), n.d. — R / K–3 / S

This "ABC" book uses alliterative types of words and phrases for each letter of the Spanish alphabet.

Galarza, Ernesto. *Más poemas párvulos.* San Jose: Editorial Almaden, 1972. — R / K–3 / S

Several Mexican versions of Mother Goose are presented.

Guillen, Nicolas. *Por el mar de las antillas anda un barco de papel.* Illustrated by Horacio Elena. Unión de Escritores y Artistas de Cuba, 1978. — R / 4–6 / S

This collection of poems includes a series of riddles and poems about a pair of enchanting characters, Sapito and Sapon, through which the author achieves amazingly musical effects. It is beautifully illustrated.

Uribe, Maria de la Luz. *Cuenta que te cuento.* Illustrated by Fernando Krahn. Juventud, 1979 (distributed by Donars). — C / 4–6 / S

The five stories in verse are humorous and lighthearted. In the first one, *El rey de papel,* a young girl visits a unique kingdom where everything, including the king and his ten little princesses, are made of paper.

	Type of entry	Grade level	Language

Vega, Blanca de la. *Antología de la poesía infantil.* Buenos Aires: Editorial Kapelusz, 1960. — C | 4–6 | S

This anthology of poetry includes classic works as well as poems of a didactic and moralistic nature. The print is very small.

Walsh, Maria Elena. *Tutu maramba.* Illustrated by Vilar. Editorial Sudamericana, 1977. — R | 4–6 | S

The author's ability to play with images and sounds makes her poetry popular. Some of her best-loved poems come from this book.

Contemporary Realistic Fiction

Burningham, John. *Harquin: El zorro que baja al valle.* Miñon, 1964. — R | 4–6 | S

A fox, Harquin, whose parents have told their children not to go beyond the valley, is fascinated by the idea of discovering what lies beyond and makes trips to town. When he is seen, a hunt is organized, and he realizes he has endangered his family.

Hahn, Jae Hyun. *Seven Korean Sisters.* The Institute for Intercultural Studies, Los Angeles, 1980. — C | 1–5 | K

The origin of the sakdong chogori worn by Korean girls and women on special days is explained in this fanciful story.

Hahn, Jae Hyun, and Han Hahn. *Special Korean Birthday.* The Institute for Intercultural Studies, Los Angeles, 1980. — C | 1–3 | K

Young Soo, a Korean immigrant boy, invites his friend Paul to his baby sister's first birthday party. The sister receives many gifts and is seated at her birthday table with the objects and food. Paul comes to understand the significance of the gifts and to appreciate his friend's Korean heritage.

Hien, Nguyen Thai Duc. *Doi song moi/Tren dat moi: A New Life in a New Land.* National Assessment and Dissemination Center, 1980. — C | 3–6 | V

This fourth-grade reader is for Vietnamese students trying to adjust to a new life in America. The stories, using members of the Nam family as the central figures, highlight American and Vietnamese customs. The last chapter presents several Vietnamese folktales.

Kurusa. *La calle es libre.* Illustrated by Monika Doppert. Caracas: Ediciones Ekare-Banco del Libro, 1981. — R | 4–6 | S

Poor children try to obtain a playground in which to play.

Paz, Marcela. *Papelucho* (and 11 other titles). Santiago de Chile: Editorial Universitaria, 1979. — R | 4–6 | S

Humorous situations are created when Papelucho uses his imagination to act out his fantasies.

Pellicer Lopez, Carlos. *Juan y sus zapatos.* Promociones Editoriales Mexicanas, 1982. — R | K–3 | S

A lonely boy's shoes talk to him about the wonderful sights they have viewed during the boy's dreams.

	Type of entry	Grade level	Language

Velthuys, Max. *El gentíl dragón rojo.* Valladolid: Miñon, 1975.

> When the red dragon is captured, different opinions are expressed: the mob wants to kill him; the scientist wants to preserve him; a general attempts to transform him into a fighting force; and finally he is exhibited in jail. A happy solution is found.

R / 4–6 / S

Historical Fiction

Aquilera, Carmen. *Citlalli y las estrellas.* Illustrated by Jeanne Robledo. Organización Editorial Novaro, 1982.

> Citlalli is a young girl living in fifteenth-century Mexico. One night she is allowed to travel through the skies to visit her mother, who has died and is a star at night and a maiden of the sun by day.

R / 4–6 / S

Cardenas, Magolo. *Celestino y el tren.* Illustrated by Gerardo Cantu. Organización Editorial Novaro, 1982.

> A young boy joins his father on a trip to the city. They are carrying merchandise on their burros, and the trip is full of adventure. The illustrations are beautiful.

R / 4–6 / S

De la Vara, Armida. *El tronaviaje.* Illustrated by Fiona Alexander. Organización Editorial Novaro, 1982.

> A friar, Andrés de Urdaneta, travels from Mexico to the Philippines. His eleven-year-old nephew, Andresito, manages to board the ship, and it is through the boy's eyes that we witness the adventure.

R / 4–6 / S

McCunn, Ruthanne L. *Pie-Biter* (Chinese edition *Pai wanga hai*). Design Enterprises of San Francisco, 1983.

> Hoi was a small, skinny Chinese boy when he came to America to help build the railroads. His love for American pies wins him the nickname of "Pie-Biter."

R / 4–8 / C

Medero, Marines. *Al otro lado de la puerta.* Illustrated by Claudio Isaac. Organización Editorial Novaro, 1982.

> Ana lives in eighteenth-century Mexico. She discovers that life in the streets and in the mines is not as beautiful and protected as it is in her rich home. She discovers the concept of Mexican nationality and what liberty, equality, and fraternity really mean.

R / 4–6 / S

Nonfiction—Information

Macaulay, David. *Grandes creaciones del hombre.* Houghton, 1977.

> This is a Spanish translation of David Macaulay's books on the building of hypothetical structures. The collection includes *Castle, Cathedral, City, Pyramid,* and *Underground.*

R / 4–8 / S

Mitgutsch, Ali. *De la arcilla al ladrillo* (and other titles). Carolrhoda Books, Inc., 1970s to 1980s.

> This is a translation into Spanish of a series of start-to-finish books, including *From Clay to Bricks.* There are over 20 English titles listed, including *Cement to Bridge, Cow to Shoe, Egg to Bird, Oil to Gasoline,* and *Ore to Spoon.*

R / K–3 / S

	Type of entry	Grade level	Language

Yee, Diane C. *Gung hay fat choy.* Children's Press, 1981.

| | C | K–3 | C |

The author explains the significance of the Chinese New Year and describes its celebration by Chinese Americans.

Plays

Armijo, Carmen. *Bim, bam, bom (arriba el telón).* Editorial Miñon, 1981.

| | C | K–3 | S |

This collection includes plays for young children. The plays are vivacious, humorous, and of adequate length to be staged. They also make good reading.

DePaola, Tomie. *Representación navideña.* Editorial Miñon, 1981.

| | C | K–3 | S |

This story of the Nativity is simplified and modernized to match the children's language.

Gimenez Pastor, Marta. *¡Respetable público!* Libreria Huemul, 1974.

| | C | 4–6 | S |

This volume consists of six scripts for puppet shows that are fun to read and present.

THE WAY FOR PARENTS TO HELP THEIR CHILDREN BECOME BETTER READERS IS TO READ TO THEM—EVEN WHEN THEY ARE VERY YOUNG.

RECREATIONAL AND MOTIVATIONAL MATERIALS

This section presents a list of recreational and motivational materials. Teachers and members of selection committees for school districts' materials can use the list to select books for students' independent reading. The list includes titles that should accommodate the broad range of reading interests of the children. The literary contributions of specific ethnic or cultural groups are identified by one of the following symbols:

B — Black
C — Chinese
F — Filipino
H — Hispanic

I — American Indian
J — Japanese
K — Korean
V — Vietnamese

In the case of books about American Indians, the tribe, group, or band dealt with in the book is designated after each title.

Picture Books

	Grade span	Culture

Alexander, Martha. *Bobo's Dream.* Dial Press, 1970. — K–2

A boy rescues his dog's bone from a larger dog. While napping, the grateful pet dreams of protecting his boy. In the dream he is a large, fierce dog; when he wakes, he is so confident that he frightens the big dog away.

Allard, Harry, and James Marshall. *Miss Nelson Is Missing.* Houghton, 1977. — 2–5

When Miss Nelson's students in Room 207 misbehave, she disappears and is replaced by a martinet, Miss Viola Swamp, much to the dismay of the children. Miss Swamp is, in reality, Miss Nelson in disguise. In time, she returns to a happy and appreciative class!

Anno, Mitsumasa. *Anno's Alphabet: An Adventure in Imagination.* Harper Junior Books, 1975. — K–3

This unusual and distinctive alphabet book shows letters as pieces of rough-grained wood and, on the opposite pages, objects beginning with that letter. It is an excellent introduction to art as well!

Anno, Mitsumasa. *Anno's Counting House.* Putnam, 1982. — K–3

This appealing book presents numbers in which the same landscapes are used throughout; houses, birds, trees, and people are added as seasons progress.

Aruego, José. *Look What I Can Do.* Scribner, 1971. — K–3

The book gently and indirectly teases children's show-off tendencies by having two animals compete in a follow-the-leader spree. At the end they are panting with fatigue, but they rouse themselves to sit on a third animal which says, "Look what I can do!"

Benchley, Nathaniel. *Oscar Otter.* Harper Junior Books, 1966. — 1–3

This story involves a young otter and his desire to get even with a beaver which has inadvertently inconvenienced him. His antics, performed against the better judgment of his father, almost prove to be disastrous. However, right wins out in the end.

Bonsall, Crosby N. *The Case of the Cat's Meow.* Harper, 1965. — 1–3

In this mystery story a cat disappears, and readers can appreciate both the humor of the situation and the satisfying outcome.

Briggs, Raymond. *The Snowman.* Random House, 1978. — K–3

In this wordless and ultimately sad story, a snowman comes alive but is all too mortal.

Brown, Marcia. *All Butterflies: An ABC.* Scribner, 1974. — K–2

Two letters are combined on each double-paged spread of this book, which the author has illustrated with woodcuts in subdued colors.

Brown, Margaret W. *Fox Eyes.* Illustrated by Garth Williams. Pantheon Books, 1951. — K–3

A red fox spies on various creatures and notes their secrets. The concerned animals are not aware that when the fox goes on his way, he promptly forgets what he has observed. He keeps this secret to himself! The book has distinctive illustrations.

Brown, Margaret W. *The Runaway Bunny.* Harper Junior Books, 1942, 1972. — K–3

When a little bunny tells his mother he is going to run away, his mother answers by telling him how she will find him.

	Grade span	Culture

Burningham, John. *Mr. Gumpy's Outing*. Holt, 1971. **K–2**

Mr. Gumpy's boat ride is disrupted by the antics of the dog, cat, rabbit, and other animals, plus two children, who ask to come along.

Burton, Virginia L. *Mike Mulligan and His Steam Shovel*. Houghton, 1943. **K–2**

When there does not seem to be much work for Mike Mulligan and his steam shovel, Mary Anne, he decides to dig a cellar for the town hall in Popperville in just one day. Can he do it? He does and finds a home for himself and Mary Anne.

Carle, Eric. *Do You Want to Be My Friend?* Harper Junior Books, 1987. **K–2**

In this almost wordless picture book, a little mouse searches for a friend among many animals.

Chenery, Janet. *The Toad Hunt*. Illustrated by Ben Shecter. Harper Junior Books, 1967. **1–3**

Teddy and Peter search for a toad and find pollywogs, frogs, a turtle, and a salamander.

Clifton, Lucille. *Amifika*. Illustrated by Thomas Di Grazia, Dutton, 1977. **1–3 B**

A young black boy's father is returning home from the army. The boy worries that his father will not remember him and that he will be "cleared" out when his mother readies the house for the return.

Clifton, Lucille. *Some of the Days of Everett Anderson*. Illustrated by Evaline Ness Holt. Holt, 1970. **K–2 B**

This is the story of a week in the life of six-year-old Everett Anderson. In verse we go from "Monday Morning Good Morning" to "Sunday Morning Lonely."

Cohen, Miriam. *Will I Have a Friend?* Macmillan, 1967. **K–1**

In this story of a boy's first day at school, he searches for a friend and experiences a typical school day.

De Brunhoff, Jean. *The Story of Babar*. Random House, 1933, 1960. **1–3**

A young elephant ventures to the big city after the death of his mother. He is adopted by a rich woman and grows fond of city ways, but he eventually returns to the forest.

Eichenberg, Fritz. *Ape in a Cape: An Alphabet of Odd Animals*. Harcourt, 1952. **1–4**

In this alphabet book each letter is represented by an animal whose name begins with that letter. A phrase for each letter includes the animal's name and a rhyming word.

Goodall, John S. *The Adventures of Paddy Pork*. Harcourt, 1968. **1–4**

While shopping with his mother, a pig runs away to find a traveling circus. His adventures eventually lead him to a disaster. The story concludes with the eventual happy reunion with his mother.

	Grade span	Culture

Hoban, Russell. *A Baby Sister for Frances.* Harper Junior Books, 1964. — K–3

Frances is feeling sad because the new baby in the badger family is taking so much of her parents' time. She decides to run away but soon discovers that her parents miss her even with a new baby in the family.

Hoban, Russell. *A Bargain for Frances.* Harper Junior Books, 1970. — 1–3

Frances, the badger, is going to Thelma's house for a tea party. Her mother reminds her to be careful because she always gets the worst of it when she plays with Thelma. Frances is not careful.

Hoban, Tana. *Look Again.* Macmillan, 1971. — 2–6

This book of photos has two-inch cut-out squares that reveal a portion of something larger on the following page. The complete picture is shown on this page with yet another view of the object on the following page.

Hoban, Tana. *Push Pull, Empty Full: A Book of Opposites.* Macmillan, 1972. — K–3

This is a short text with black-and-white photographs that illustrate 15 pairs of opposites.

Kellogg, Steven. *Pinkerton, Behave!* Dial Books, 1979. — K–2

Pinkerton, a large dog, seems to be untrainable. Actually, he responds consistently to the wrong commands at obedience school. However, when a burglar enters his home, his owner remembers Pinkerton's idiosyncrasies and all ends well.

Knight, Hilary. *Hilary Knight's the Twelve Days of Christmas.* Macmillan, 1987. — K–3

This is the traditional Christmas song nicely illustrated by the author with a bear as the central character.

Lexau, Joan M. *Benjie on His Own.* Dial Books, 1970. — K–2 B

A shy Harlem boy who lives with his grandmother is ashamed that she insists on bringing him to school and back. One afternoon she fails to pick him up, and Benjie struggles to find his way home. There he finds his grandmother desperately ill. No one is home to help, and Benjie must get his grandmother to the hospital.

Matsuno, Masako. *A Pair of Red Clogs.* Illustrated by Kazue Mizumura. World, 1960. — K–2 J

Mako's mother buys her a beautiful pair of red lacquered clogs. Mako cracks them playing a game. She wants new clogs so much that she almost does a dishonest thing to get them.

Mayer, Mercer. *Ah-Choo.* Dial, 1976. — K–2

When an elephant has to sneeze, his terrific blast has consequences for everyone.

Mayer, Mercer. *A Boy, a Dog and a Frog.* Dial, 1967. — K–3

This is a humorous, wordless book that tells the story of a little boy who sets forth with his dog and a net to catch an enterprising, personable frog.

	Grade span	Culture

McCloskey, Robert. *Time of Wonder.* Viking, 1957. — **3–6**

This example of writing and illustrating depicts ordinary life on an island in Maine. The author rhythmically conveys his love of nature and the seasonal occurrences of New England.

McPhail, David. *Pig Pig Grows Up.* Dutton, 1980. — **K–2**

Pig Pig has an overly indulgent mother, and he finds growing up very difficult. Circumstances bring him an opportunity to show his abilities, which prove his maturity. The story is funny, and the pictures are charming.

Minarik, Else H. *Little Bear.* Illustrated by Maurice Sendak. Harper Junior Books, 1978. — **K–1**

Little Bear is a charming creature that has an especially warm relationship with his mother. Little Bear wants his mother to make him a fur coat for winter. He then discovers that his own fur coat is sufficient.

Munari, Bruno. *Bruno Munari's ABC.* Collins, 1980. — **K–1**

This author-illustrated alphabet book has easily identifiable pictures. The pictures are done in bold colors with clean lines. Although the book is simple, it should provide a delightful experience for beginning readers.

Raskin, Ellen. *Spectacles.* Illustrated by Ellen Raskin. Atheneum, 1968. — **2–5**

Iris is nearsighted and is sure she sees things that really are not there. She sees a fire-breathing dragon, a giant pygmy nuthatch, and a chestnut. Iris hates glasses but gets them anyway.

Reiss, John J. *Numbers.* Bradbury Press, 1971. — **K–2**

This big and colorful counting book leads young readers from 1 to 10, then 10 to 100, and finally to 1,000. The colorful and clear drawings entice the reader to participate in the counting of the objects.

Rey, Hans A. *Curious George.* Houghton, 1941. — **K–3**

Curious George is a small monkey that has great difficulty getting used to city life before he goes to the zoo. The colored pictures, simple text, and humor of the story make it a great favorite with young readers.

Sendak, Maurice. *The Sign on Rosie's Door.* Harper Junior Books, 1960. — **K–3**

A young Brooklyn girl entertains herself and her friends on a dull summer day by putting on a show.

Seuss, Dr. *Horton Hears a Who.* Random House, 1954. — **2–5**

This is Dr. Seuss's richly inventive nonsense story of an elephant that just knew there were people living on a speck of dust that floated before his eyes. Horton convinces his skeptical jungle neighbors of the truth of his sighting.

Shecter, Ben. *Conrad's Castle.* Harper Junior Books, 1967. — **1–4**

Conrad builds a castle in the air in spite of the interruptions caused by his friends.

	Grade span	Culture

Spier, Peter. *Noah's Ark.* Doubleday, 1977. **K–3**

The biblical story of Noah and the ark is done in an artistic, almost wordless style.

Spier, Peter. *Peter Spier's Rain.* Doubleday, 1982. **K–3**

Two children explore their neighborhood in a rainstorm and then hurry home where it is warm and dry. The next morning they wake to clear skies in this wordless picture book.

Steig, William. *Amos and Boris.* Farrar, 1971. **K–2**

When Amos, a young mouse, falls off his boat, he is rescued by Boris the Whale. Amos promises to help Boris if the whale ever needs assistance, which he does.

Udry, Janice M. *A Tree Is Nice.* Harper Junior Books, 1956. **K–3**

This story is about the wonder of trees, the reasons they are important to people, and the many kinds of fun they afford us.

Van Allsburg, Chris. *Mysteries of Harris Burdick.* Houghton, 1984. **2–5**

Intriguing titles and brief lines of text invite the reader to invent stories to explain each illustration.

Waber, Bernard. *Anteater Named Arthur.* Illustrated by Bernard Waber. Houghton, 1967. **2–4**

Arthur is a problem to his mother because he questions why he is called an anteater, becomes choosy about his food, and is very forgetful. His room is more than his mother can believe.

Wagner, Jenny. *John Brown, Rose and the Midnight Cat.* Illustrated by Ron Brooks. Bradbury Press, 1977. **K–4**

An elderly widow and her big sheep dog love and care for each other. Their comfortable life is disrupted when an arrogant black cat appears on the scene.

Ward, Lynd. *The Silver Pony: A Story in Pictures.* Houghton, 1973. **4–6**

A farm boy dreams of a winged silver pony that carries him away on a series of adventures. This is a story without words.

Willard, Nancy. *Simple Pictures Are Best.* Illustrated by Tomie DePaola. Harcourt, 1978. **K–2**

The shoemaker and his wife debate over what they will wear and what will be included in their anniversary picture.

Zolotow, Charlotte. *The Quarreling Book.* Harper Junior Books, 1963. **K–3**

A family suffers through a disagreeable rainy day, but all ends well when the father returns home happy.

Folklore

Bawden, Nina. *William Tell.* Illustrated by Pascale Allamand. Lothrop, 1981. **5–6**

William Tell, a brave archer, questions Gessler's rule. Through an encounter William Tell proves his heroism.

	Grade span	Culture

Baylor, Byrd. *They Put on Masks.* Scribner, 1974. — **3–6** | **I**

Through free verse and illustrations, the use and meaning of ceremonial Indian masks is explained. Related tribal legends and charts are included.

Belting, Natalia M. *Whirlwind Is a Ghost Dancing.* Dutton, 1974. — **5–9** | **I**

The thoughts of the American Indian are expressed briefly and poetically as he speaks about the world around him.

Bernstein, Margery, and Janet Kobrin. *Coyote Goes Hunting for Fire: A California Indian Myth* (Yana, California). Scribner, 1974. — **K–3** | **I**

As all the other animals fear, Coyote successfully bungles their plans to obtain fire.

Bryant, Sara Cone. *The Burning Rice Fields.* Holt, 1963. — **3–6**

An old Japanese man sacrifices his rice field by setting it on fire to warn the villagers of the coming tidal wave.

Courlander, Harold. *The Crest and the Hide and Other African Stories.* Coward, 1982. — **4–6** | **B**

This is a collection of tales of deeds performed by the noble men of Africa with notes on the background of each story.

D'Aulaire, Ingri, and Edgar D'Aulaire. *D'Aulaires' Trolls.* Doubleday, 1972. — **4–6**

Children will revel in the glorious array of forest trolls, water and sea trolls, little mischievous gnome-trolls, and the biggest, most nightmarish of all, the mountain trolls. The illustrations are alive with vigor.

De Angeli, Marguerite. *Marguerite De Angeli's Book of Nursery and Mother Goose Rhymes.* Doubleday, 1954. — **K–2**

Marguerite De Angeli has compiled and illustrated a beautiful edition that offers nearly 400 rhymes, including all the old favorites and some that are not so familiar, plus over 250 pictures.

DePaola, Tomie. *The Lady of Guadalupe.* Holiday House, 1980. — **4–6** | **H**

This story is a simply told and well-developed narrative about an Indian peasant who was visited by the Virgin Mary in 1531 and instructed to tell the bishop of Mexico to build a church in her honor. The sign that she provided became the source of the legend of the patron saint of Mexico.

Domanska, Janina. *The Turnip.* Macmillan, 1969. — **2–4**

Grandfather planted a turnip, and Grandmother watered it every day. The turnip grew and grew and grew.

Farmer, Penelope. *Daedalus and Icarus.* Illustrated by Chris Connor. Harcourt, 1971. — **4–6**

This is a retelling of the Greek myth of man's first attempt to fly.

The Fire Plume: Legends of the American Indians. Edited by John Bierhorst and Henry Rowe Schoolcraft. Dial Press, 1969. — **4–6** | **I**

This book includes tales of adventure and romance of the Algonquin family of tribes of the United States and Canada, including the Chippewa, Shawnee, Ottawa, and Menominee Indians. These stories were collected by Henry Rowe Schoolcraft around 1850.

	Grade span	Culture

Fisher, Anne B. *Stories California Indians Told* (California). Houghton, 1957. — 5–9 — I

Twelve stories of California Indians relate how the Great Spirit created California; how light, fire, and the mountains were made; and how the god Coyote helped the people overcome the hardship of their lives. They are retold with animation and presented in a well-designed, effectively illustrated book.

Frasconi, Antonio. *The House That Jack Built: A Picture Book in Two Languages.* Harcourt, 1958. — K–2

On each page the lines cumulate separately in French and in English until the end of the tale is reached; then the story is reiterated, with French and English in coupled lines. In a third section questions are in English and answers are in French.

Galdone, Paul. *Old Mother Hubbard and Her Dog.* McGraw, 1960. — 1–3

The entire rhymed tale of Mother Hubbard is illustrated by Paul Galdone in lovely, humorous black-and-white pictures with touches of red. This attractive addition to Mother Goose and picture book collections can be used for reading aloud.

Gates, Doris. *The Golden God: Apollo.* Illustrated by Constantino Coconis. Viking, 1973. — 5–6

The author presents 16 stories involving Apollo, including his birth, his victory over Python, his fruitless pursuit of Daphne, the loss of his son Phaethon, and his relationship with his twin sister Artemis. Illustrations capture the horror and strength of the myths.

Gates, Doris. *Two Queens of Heaven: Aphrodite and Demeter.* Illustrated by Trina S. Hyman. Viking, 1974. — 5–7

The author retells some Greek myths in which the goddesses of love and fertility play a major role. Included are stories of Adonis, Anchises and Aphrodite, Pygmalion, Atalanta, Cupid and Psyche, Hero and Leander, Pyramus and Thisbe, Demeter and Persephone, and Aphrodite's birth from the sea foam.

Gates, Doris. *The Warrior Goddess: Athena.* Illustrated by Don Bolognese. Viking, 1972. — 5–6

This is a retelling of the story of Athena's birth, along with other myths in which the Greek goddess plays a part. Included are stories about Aglauros, Perseus, Medusa, Andromeda, Bellerophon, Jason, Heracles, Medea, and Arachne.

Goble, Paul. *The Gift of the Sacred Dog* (Plains). Bradbury Press, 1980. — K–3 — I

The author presents one of the common myths of how the Plains Indians got horses. He tells of a boy from a tribe whose members are starving because they cannot find buffalo. The boy talks to the Great Spirit and gets sacred dogs (horses) for hunting.

Goble, Paul. *Star Boy.* Bradbury Press, 1983. — 1–3

This is a retelling of the Blackfeet Indian legend of Star Boy, marked by the sun as a reminder of his mother's disobedience. Ugly and poor, Star Boy loses hope of wedding the girl he loves. She gives him the courage, however, to persevere in finding a way to Sky World, where he is given beauty and riches.

	Grade span	Culture

Grimm, Jacob, and Wilhelm Grimm. *The Fisherman and His Wife.* Translated by Elizabeth Shub and illustrated by Monika Laimgruber. Greenwillow Books, 1978.   [3–6]

A poor fisherman catches a magic fish and releases it when the fish pleads for its life. The man's wife sends him back to the fish to ask a wish in return. The fisherman continues to visit the fish with his wife's demands. Finally, she asks too much and loses everything.

Grimm, Jacob, and Wilhelm Grimm. *Grimms' Golden Goose.* Illustrated by Charles Mikolaycak. Random House, 1969.   [3–5]

The princess laughs at seven people stuck to the Simpleton's golden goose, but the king demands that the Simpleton perform three impossible tasks before claiming the princess as his wife.

Grimm, Jacob, and Wilhelm Grimm. *The Seven Ravens.* Translated by Elizabeth D. Crawford and illustrated by Lisbeth Zwerger. Morrow, 1981.   [4–6]

Seven brothers are changed into coal-black ravens after they fail to return from fetching water for their sister's christening quickly enough to satisfy their father. The sister sets out to undo the terrible magic.

Guy, Rosa. *Mother Crocodile: An Uncle Amadou Tale from Senegal.* Delacorte Press, 1981.   [4–6]

The old storyteller, Uncle Amadou, says that Mother Crocodile probably has the best memory on earth, but her children believe Golo the Monkey when he says that she is crazy, and they ignore her when she warns that they should learn from past experience. Only through recalling Mother Crocodile's stories are they able to save their skins.

Hague, Kathleen, and Michael Hague. *The Man Who Kept House.* Illustrated by Michael Hague. Harcourt, 1981.   [K–3]

A husband and wife trade jobs when the husband accuses his wife of doing little and being poorly organized. He soon learns and never complains again.

Hap, Le Huy. *Vietnamese Legends.* Tuttle, 1965.   [3–8] [V]

The author, a former director of the Vietnamese-American Association, adapted these traditional Indo-Chinese tales.

Highwater, Jamake. *Anpao: An American Indian Odyssey* (Northern Plains). Lippincott, 1977.   [6–9] [I]

Anpao's many adventures include encounters with the white man and his guns, horses, and diseases. The heritage of American Indians is described.

Hillerman, Tony. *The Boy Who Made Dragonfly.* Harper Junior Books, 1972.   [6–9] [I]

A boy, left behind when his village moves to a better place, not only protects his sister but also creates a dragonfly. This creature comes to life and helps the boy. Eventually, the boy and his people learn how valuable good manners are.

	Grade span	Culture

Hirsch, Marilyn. *Could Anything Be Worse?* Holiday House, 1974. — 3-6

A man complains constantly about his family. When he asks the rabbi for advice, the wise man suggests he bring his chickens, cow, and relatives into his home. When the man finally gets rid of the animals and the relatives, his home seems utterly peaceful, and he no longer complains about his family.

Hodges, Margaret. *The Fire Bringer: A Paiute Indian Legend* (Paiute). Little, 1972. — K-4, I

An Indian boy observes to his companion, a coyote, that his people are very cold in the winter. The coyote offers to obtain fire for the people. The people call the boy Fire Bringer; after the boy dies, the coyote is called the Fire Bringer, and he has markings on his sides to prove it.

Hogrogian, Nonny. *Always Room for One More.* Holt, 1965. — K-5

Lachie MacLachlan is a generous man who takes anyone into his home. So many people come that the house overflows. The friends put up a new, bigger house so that Lachie can always have room for one more.

Kroeber, Theodora. *The Inland Whale: Nine Stories Retold from California Indian Legends* (California). University of California Press, 1959. — 6-9, I

These nine stories that are retold from California Indian legends bring the oral literature of primitive peoples into the realm of literature.

LeCain, Errol. *The Twelve Dancing Princesses.* Illustrated by Errol LeCain. Viking, 1978. — 3-5

A king has 12 beautiful daughters who obviously dance all night, for their shoes are worn out every morning. No one can discover how this happens until a poor soldier, who is given a magic cloak, arrives. His reward is to marry the daughter of his choice.

The Lion and the Rat: A Fable by La Fontaine. Illustrated by Brian Wildsmith. Watts, 1963. — 2-6

A lion learns, happily, that a kindness is never wasted in this dramatically illustrated telling of the fable.

Lobel, Anita. *The Pancake.* William Morrow, 1978. — K-3

In this Gingerbread-Boy-type story, a rolling pancake eludes all its pursuers except one clever pig.

Malcolmson, Anne. *Yankee Doodle's Cousins.* Houghton, 1941. — 4-6

This collection of American literature includes 27 legends, tall tales, and stories that highlight a variety of heroes.

Merrill, Jean. *The Superlative Horse.* William R. Scott, 1961. — 5-6, C

This is the moving story of a young boy who earns the position and honor of selecting horses for the finest stable in all of China. It is based on a Taoist story written about 350 B.C.

	Grade span	Culture

The Miller, the Boy and the Donkey. Adapted and illustrated by Brian Wildsmith. Watts, 1969. — 3–6

In this colorful Wildsmith rendition of a La Fontaine fable, the miller takes the advice of a variety of people on how to transport his donkey to market.

Montgomery, Jean. ***The Wrath of Coyote*** (California). William Morrow, 1968. — 6–9 | I

This novel, which is based on the life of the legendary Chief Marin, describes the conflict between Spanish settlers and the California Indians who inhabited the area of present-day San Francisco.

The Mother Goose Treasury. Edited and illustrated by Raymond Briggs. Coward, 1966. — K–4

This book of nursery rhymes is illustrated in black and white as well as color.

Nguyen, Lan. ***Vietnamese Folktales.*** Office of the Alameda County Superintendent of Schools, 1981. — 3–8 | V

This book contains four stories titled "Betel Leaves and the Areca Nut," "The Gold Coins," "The Heart of Jade," and "The New Year's Delicacies."

Politi, Leo. ***Pedro, the Angel of Olvera Street.*** Scribner, 1946. — 2–4 | H

This delightful picture book tells the story of the Mexican Christmas celebration known as the Posada procession.

Ransome, Arthur. ***The Fool of the World and the Flying Ship.*** Illustrated by Uri Shulevitz. Farrar, 1968. — 1–3

This vividly illustrated Russian folktale is about a peasant who marries the Czar's daughter after overcoming many obstacles with the help of a wise old man and seven unusual companions.

Reeves, James. ***The Trojan Horse.*** Watts, 1968. — 5–6

A ten-year-old child tells the tale of the Trojan Horse and how the people of Troy were tricked by the Greeks.

The Riddle of the Drum: A Tale from Tizapan, Mexico. Retold by Verna Aardema and illustrated by Tony Chen. Four Winds Press, 1979. — 2–4 | H

Anxious to keep his daughter from marrying, a king announces that no man may marry her unless he guesses the kind of leather used in a drum made by a wizard. Prince Tuzan succeeds.

Sewell, Helen, and Thomas Bullfinch. ***A Book of Myths.*** Illustrated by Helen Sewell. Macmillan, 1942. — 5–8

This selection of favorite myths includes stories of Cupid and Psyche, Venus and Adonis, the Golden Fleece, Hero and Leander, Hercules, Theseus, Midas, the Apple of Discord, and many others.

Shulevitz, Uri. ***The Magician: An Adaptation from the Yiddish of I. L. Peretz.*** Macmillan, 1973. — 5–7

The magician appears on the eve of Passover and conjures a feast for a pious but needy couple. The couple realizes that the magician was Elijah himself.

	Grade span	Culture

Singer, Isaac B. *Naftali the Storyteller and His Horse, Sus.* Farrar, 1976. **4–6**

This collection of stories includes "The Fools of Chelm and the Stupid Carp" in which a carp is to be sentenced for slapping the face of one of the town's community leaders.

Small, Ernest, and Blair Lent. *Baba Yaga.* Houghton, 1966. **4–6**

Baba Yaga tries to make little Russian Marusia into stew when she is found in the forest looking for turnips. Marusia and the hedgehog match wits with Baba Yaga.

Stamm, Claus. *Three Strong Women: A Tall Tale from Japan.* Viking, 1962. **3–5** J

In this humorous tale three strong women take Forever Mountain into training so that he might win the prize money wrestling before the emperor.

Stevenson, James. *Could Be Worse!* Greenwillow, 1977. **2–5**

Everything is always the same at Grandpa's house—until one unusual morning. Grandpa relates his interesting adventure only to have his favorite saying come back to him.

Thong, Le Tinh. *Popular Stories from Vietnam.* Institute for Cultural Pluralism, San Diego State University, 1977. **4–8** V

These stories were rewritten in simple English by Vietnamese teachers studying at the English Language Institute, Victoria University, Wellington, New Zealand.

Toye, William. *The Loon's Necklace* (Tsimshian). Oxford University Press, 1977. **K–3** I

A blind old man asks wise Loon for advice when an old hag causes trouble. He repays Loon's gift of sight with a necklace that causes the markings on the bird's feathers.

Uchida, Yoshiko. *Sea of Gold and Other Tales from Japan.* Scribner, 1965. **1–4** J

These Japanese folktales of clever and foolish animals and people illustrate that those with kind hearts will be rewarded.

Whitney, Alex. *Stiff Ears: Animal Folktales of the North American Indian.* Walck, 1974. **2–4**

Taken from the folklore of six North American tribes, these short, easy-to-read stories feature animal heroes. Brief notes on the Indian way of life are included.

Who's in Rabbit's House. Retold by Verna Aardema. Dial, 1977; Pied Piper, 1979. **2–5** B

This Masai tale is presented in the form of a play. The frog gets the job of getting a monster out of the rabbit's house. The leopard, elephant, and rhino bungle the job.

Wiesner, William. *Turnabout.* Seabury Press, 1972. **3–6**

In this Norwegian folktale a farmer swaps jobs with his wife and discovers that housekeeping is not an easy job.

	Grade span	Culture

Yolen, Jane. *The Emperor and the Kite.* Philomel, 1967. — 3–6

In this retelling of a Chinese tale, a princess, smallest in her family, is ignored by her father and brothers. She becomes interested in kites and uses a kite to help her father escape from a tower after he is imprisoned by bad men.

Zemach, Harve. *Nail Soup.* Follett, 1964. — 3–6

Two hungry travelers trick the townspeople in a small village by claiming to be able to create a delicious soup using only water and a nail.

Modern Fantasy and Science Fiction

Alexander, Lloyd. *The Wizard in the Tree.* Illustrated by Laszlo Kubinyi. Dutton, 1974. — 5–6

An overworked servant girl with a faith in magic frees an enchanter from his centuries-long imprisonment in an oak tree. The enchanter creates havoc, because he is unable to control his magical powers as he tries to transport himself to where his peers are.

Andersen, Hans Christian. *The Steadfast Tin Soldier.* Illustrated by Thomas Di Grazia. Prentice-Hall, 1981. — 5–8

A one-legged toy soldier, after being accidentally launched on a dangerous voyage, finds his way back to his true love, a dancing girl made of paper.

Andersen, Hans Christian. *Thumbelina.* Illustrated by Elizabeth Zwerger. Morrow, 1980. — 3–5

A tiny girl becomes queen of all the flowers after being kidnapped by an ugly toad.

Barrie, James. *Peter Pan.* Edited and illustrated by Noras Unwin. Scribner, 1950. — 5–8

This book describes the adventures of Peter Pan, a boy who refuses to grow up.

Baum, L. Frank. *The Wizard of Oz.* Illustrated by Michael Hague. Holt, 1982. — 4–8

When Dorothy is transported to the Land of Oz by a cyclone, she must find the great wizard in order to return home to Kansas.

Burnett, Frances H. *The Secret Garden.* Lippincott, 1962, 1965. — 4–8

Ten-year-old Mary comes to live in a lonely house on the Yorkshire moors and discovers the mysteries of a locked garden.

Burton, Virginia L. *Katy and the Big Snow.* Houghton, 1943. — 1–3

Katy, a tractor, saves the city when it is snowed in by a blizzard.

Butterworth, Oliver. *The Enormous Egg.* Illustrated by Louis Darling. Little, 1956. — 4–6

When Nate, a New Hampshire boy, looks in the henhouse, he is not prepared to see the biggest egg he has ever seen. No one is prepared for what hatches out of that enormous egg!

	Grade span	Culture

Cameron, Eleanor. *The Wonderful Flight to the Mushroom Planet*. Illustrated by Robert Henneberger. Little, 1954. **3-5**

David, always dreaming of cruising the solar system in his own space-ship, enlists his friend Chuck to help build the spaceship. A great adventure with the Mushroom Grower follows.

Cassedy, Sylvia. *Behind the Attic Wall*. Harper Junior Books, 1983. **5-6**

A neglected Maggie, living in a bleak old house with her great-aunts, hears ghostly voices and finds the magic that helps her to love and to be loved.

Christopher, John. *The Pool of Fire*. Macmillan, 1968; Collier, 1970. **6-8**

The reader is caught up in a race against time in this suspenseful story, the third in the author's trilogy.

Cleary, Beverly. *The Mouse and the Motorcycle*. Illustrated by Louis Darling. William Morrow, 1965. **4-5**

In this fantasy a mouse named Ralph learns to ride a motorcycle. Keith, the owner of the motorcycle, becomes Ralph's friend and defends him when danger comes.

Cooper, Susan. *Greenwitch*. Harcourt, 1974. **6-8**

The Servants of Light struggle with the Powers of Darkness.

Cooper, Susan. *The Grey King*. Macmillan, 1975. **6-8**

In this Arthurian fantasy the author describes the experiences of Will Stanton, Bran the sheep dog, and the ghostly grey foxes that are drawn together in an epic struggle of a world beyond time.

Erickson, Russell. *A Toad for Tuesday*. Illustrated by Lawrence DiFiori. Lothrop, 1974. **K-2**

Warton the toad goes on skis to visit his aunt. On the way he rescues a mouse from danger and is captured by an owl that threatens to eat him.

Fatio, Louise. *The Happy Lion*. Illustrated by Roger Duvoisin. McGraw-Hill, 1954. **K-2**

When a lion in the Paris zoo escapes, he is no longer everybody's favorite! His only friend, a little boy, leads him back to his cage.

Godden, Rumer. *The Doll's House*. Illustrated by Tasha Tudor. Puffin Books, 1947, 1976. **4-6**

First published in England, this story is about a brave little 100-year-old Dutch doll, her family, their Victorian dollhouse home, and the two little English girls to whom they belong.

Godden, Rumer. *The Mousewife*. Illustrated by Heidi Holder. Viking, 1951, 1982. **1-4**

This fantasy is notable for its subtle wit and its championing of women. Even though Mousewife has a large family to care for, she finds time to dream and help others.

Guilfoile, Elizabeth. *Nobody Listens to Andrew*. Follett, 1957. **K-4**

When friends and family finally get around to listening to Andrew, they discover he really does have something important to say.

	Grade span	Culture

Han, Mieko. ***Turtle Power—Chinese.*** National Asian Center for Bilingual Education, 1983.   **1–6**   **C**

Every page of this Vietnamese folktale is in English and Vietnamese. A turtle saves the life of the Dragon King, which lives in the sea, by going ashore and bringing back ginseng to heal the king.

Hoban, Russell. ***Nothing to Do.*** Illustrated by Lillian Hoban. Harper Junior Books, 1964.   **K–3**

When Walter Possum has nothing to do and cannot think of anything to do, Father gives him a something-to-do stone. It works for Walter. Even after he loses the stone, he not only is able to think of things to do for himself and his friend but also he gives his tag-along sister a play-right-here stick.

Hoff, Syd. ***Danny and the Dinosaur.*** Harper Junior Books, 1958.   **1–3**

In this *I Can Read Book,* Danny visits the museum and finds a dinosaur that goes all over town with him, helping people and playing games with Danny's friends before he has to return to the museum.

Howe, Deborah, and James Howe. ***Bunnicula: A Rabbit Tale of Mystery.*** Atheneum, 1980.   **1–5**

Harold the dog tells this story about the strange rabbit found by his family at the movie *Dracula.* Chester the cat suspects something is wrong when white vegetables, drained dry and with two fang marks in them, are found. Besides, Bunnicula sleeps all day and is awake at night. And he has teeth like fangs and strange markings!

Kellogg, Steven. ***The Mysterious Tadpole.*** Dial Books, 1977.   **K–3**

Louis receives a tadpole from his uncle in Scotland that does *not* become a frog; it becomes a rapidly growing "critter." Louis must find some place for his huge pet to stay, and it is his friend, the librarian, who helps figure out a solution to the problem.

Kipling, Rudyard. ***The Jungle Book.*** Children's Press, 1968.   **4–6**

Reading *The Jungle Book* is like entering a different world. Kipling makes the characters so real and three-dimensional. This particular book contains all the Mowgli stories (boy raised among the wolves) plus several others, such as the one about Rikki-Tikki-Tavi and the Elephant Boy.

Kipling, Rudyard. ***Just So Stories.*** Illustrated by Victor G. Ambrus. Rand McNally, 1982.   **4–7**

These stories tell how it was in the distant past when elephants did not have trunks, camels did not have humps, and things were not as they are now. Kipling's tales, written many years ago, are still entertaining for young children.

Kraus, Robert. ***Milton the Early Riser.*** Illustrated by José Aruego and Ariane Aruego. Messner, 1981.   **K–3**

A panda in the jungle tries to wake up all the other animals by making loud noises. As he gives up and goes to sleep, the other animals awaken.

Kraus, Robert. ***Whose Mouse Are You?*** Macmillan, 1970.   **K–2**

A young mouse, left alone when dangerous things happen to his family (for example, they are inside a cat, in a trap), rescues everybody and finds himself loved and with a family again. This is a satisfying story for young children.

	Grade span	Culture

Lindgren, Astrid. *Pippi Longstocking.* Illustrated by Louis S. Glanzman. Viking, 1950. **4–7**

Pippi Longstocking is a most unusual little girl. She lives alone, except for her monkey and her horse, because she has no father or mother. She has two red braids that stick straight out from her head, and she wears rather strange clothes. Her most amazing attribute is her strength.

Lionni, Leo. *The Biggest House in the World.* Pantheon, 1968. **K–3**

Once upon a time a little snail wanted the biggest house in the world. So his father told him a story about a snail that was able to grow the biggest house in the world, but when he did, he could not move to a new leaf with all the other snails. The little snail decided his little house was just right.

Lionni, Leo. *Inch by Inch.* Astor-Honor, 1962. **K–3**

When about to be gobbled up by the robin, the inchworm tells the bird not to eat him. The inchworm shows that he is useful and can measure things! The robin asks the inchworm to measure his tail and is very pleased with the result. The inchworm measures and measures and even tricks the nightingale by measuring.

Lobel, Arnold. *Frog and Toad Together.* Harper Junior Books, 1972. **K–3**

This *I Can Read Book* has five stories about Frog and Toad and the things they do together, such as eating cookies, being brave, and being friends. Young children like to read about these two friends because they are supportive of each other.

Milne, A. A. *Winnie-the-Pooh.* Illustrated by Ernest H. Shepard. Dutton, 1954. **3–5**

Christopher Robin lives in the wood behind the green door. Winnie-the-Pooh, his close friend, lives in the wood also, as do Piglet, Rabbit, Owl, Kanga, Little Roo, and Eeyore. The ten stories are about these friends and their adventures. The charming "decorations" by Ernest Shepard are very important to the enjoyment of this book.

Nesbit, Edith. *The Railway Children.* Coward, 1957. **3–6**

When their father is falsely imprisoned, Roberta, Peter, and Phyllis move with their mother to a simple country cottage near the railway, where they become involved in such adventures as saving a train from an accident. They also clear their father's name.

Noble, Trinka H. *The Day Jimmy's Boa Ate the Wash.* Illustrated by Steven Kellogg. Dial Books, 1980. **K–3**

"How was your field trip?" asks Mother. "Oh, boring . . . kind of dull . . . until the cow started crying," answers the little girl. The explanation of why the cow was crying goes on and on in a really funny recital of what can happen when a child takes a boa constrictor on a field trip to a farm!

Parish, Peggy. *Amelia Bedelia.* Harper Junior Books, 1963. **3–6**

In this read-along book, Amelia is left alone in the house on her first day of work. Her literal interpretation of instructions leads to hilarious happenings. Limited-English-speaking children can identify with this book.

	Grade span	Culture

Peet, Bill. *Chester the Worldly Pig.* Houghton, 1965.

2–4

Chester runs away to join a circus. When he finds that life in the big top performing with tigers does not fit his idea of fun, he happily returns home.

Peet, Bill. *Huge Harold.* Houghton, 1961.

3–5

Harold is a baby rabbit that grows to be the size of a cow. He likes being big but not that big! The story is told in verse accompanied by bold, colorful drawings and has broad appeal for children.

Seuss, Dr. *Horton Hatches the Egg.* Random House, 1940.

2–4

A bird, too lazy to sit on her own egg, asks Horton to sit while she takes a vacation. Horton sits through many hazards and is rewarded for his faithfulness.

Steig, William. *The Amazing Bone.* Farrar, 1976.

3–6

Pearl finds an unusual bone on her way home from school and discovers that it has unexpected powers.

Ungerer, Tomi. *Crictor.* Harper Junior Books, 1958.

3–6

When Madame Bodot receives a boa constrictor as a birthday present from her son in Africa, many improbable and delightful situations occur.

Poetry

Adoff, Arnold. *Sports Pages.* Lippincott Junior Books, 1986.

3–6

The feelings and experiences of young athletes are expressed in poetry as they participate in a variety of sports.

Aiken, Conrad. *Cats and Bats and Things with Wings.* Illustrated by Milton Glaser. Atheneum, 1965.

3–6

This collection of poems is about a variety of animals, all the way from the common house cat to the uncommon mandrill.

Benet, Stephen, and Rosemary Benet. *America Is Not All Traffic Lights.* Little, 1976.

3–6

Poems of the Midwest are presented.

Bodecker, N. M. *Let's Marry Said the Cherry* (and other titles). Atheneum, 1974.

2–5

The author uses word play to highlight this collection of humorous poems about absurd people and animals.

Clifton, Lucille. *Some of the Days of Everett Anderson.* Illustrated by Evaline Ness Holt. Holt, 1970.

4–6

The book includes nine poems about a lonely boy, his feelings, and the things he likes to do.

Cole, William. *Beastly Boys and Ghastly Girls.* Collins, 1964.

5–6

This is an exaggerated look at what boys and girls should never do. It is humorous and full of wit.

Cole, William. *The Birds and the Beasts Were There.* World, 1963.

K–3

This book contains a delighful collection of animal poems.

	Grade span	*Culture*

Frost, Robert. *You Come Too.* Holt, 1967.

> This book includes poems with special appeal to the youngest readers.

Grade span: 3-8

Lawrence, D. H. *Birds, Beasts and the Third Thing: Poems.* Viking, 1982.

> This collection of D. H. Lawrence's poems was selected and illustrated by Alice Provensen and Martin Provensen based on themes from the natural world.

Grade span: 4-7

Lear, Edward. *The Complete Nonsense Book.* Dodd, Mead, 1943.

> This collection of Lear's absurdities includes nonsense verse, prose, drawings, alphabet, and other rhymes.

Grade span: 2-6

Lear, Edward, and Ogden Nash. *The Scroobious Pip.* Illustrated by Nancy Ekholm Burkert. Harper Junior Books, 1968.

> This is one of Lear's most engaging poems, in which all the animals in the world gather around a strange creature that calls himself the Scroobious Pip.

Grade span: 2-6

Lee, Dennis. *Garbage Delight.* Illustrated by Frank Newfeld. Houghton, 1978.

> This is a banquet of nonsense poems to satisfy every appetite, with a beat to satisfy every drummer.

Grade span: 3-6

Livingston, Myra Cohn. *Monkey Puzzle and Other Poems.* Atheneum, 1984.

> Children will enjoy this collection of poems about trees of the United States, from the white birches in New England to the redwoods in California.

Grade span: 6-8

McCord, David. *Away and Ago.* Illustrated by Leslie Morrill. Little, 1966.

> Familiar objects, places, and experiences are described in this collection of poems.

Grade span: 4-6

Moore, Clement. *The Night Before Christmas.* Illustrated by Tomie DePaola. Holiday House, 1980.

> A mid-nineteenth century New Hampshire town is the setting for this version of Clement Moore's poem. The pages are bordered with designs from New England quilts that lend a folk quality to the story.

Grade span: 1-6

Moore, Lilian. *Go with the Poem.* McGraw-Hill, 1979.

> This contemporary anthology celebrates the city, the joy of sport, and the changing of the seasons.

Grade span: 4-6

Moore, Lilian. *See My Lovely Poison Ivy.* Illustrated by Diane Dawson. Atheneum, 1975.

> Gently ghoulish poems and drawings provide Halloween fun and any-time chuckles for young readers and listeners.

Grade span: 3-6

More Cricket Songs: Japanese Haiku. Translated by Harry Behn. Harcourt, 1971.

> This is a translation of haiku, a typical Japanese verse of three lines of five, seven, and five syllables.

Grade span: 3-6

	Grade span	Culture

On City Streets: An Anthology of Poetry. Edited by Nancy Larrick. Evans, 1968. — 5–8

This is a collection of poetry that captures the sights, sounds, and rhythms of city life. The poems are by Langston Hughes, Carl Sandburg, E. B. White, and others.

Prelutsky, Jack. ***Random House Book of Poetry for Children.*** Illustrated by Arnold Lobel. Random House, 1983. — 3–6

Jack Prelutsky writes the opening poems for each section of this book of more than 500 entries, including American, English, and anonymous works.

Sendak, Maurice. ***Pierre.*** Harper Junior Books, 1962. — 2–6

"There once was a boy named Pierre/ Who only would say, 'I don't care!'/ Read this story, my friend/ For you'll find at the end/ That a suitable moral lies there."

Silverstein, Shel. ***A Light in the Attic.*** Harper Junior Books, 1981. — 2–6

This collection contains humorous poems to be enjoyed by children and others with a funny bone.

Thayer, Ernest L. ***Casey at the Bat.*** Illustrated by Leonard E. Fisher. Watts, 1964. — 3–8

The well-known poem about the fictitious batter and his luck at the game is aptly illustrated.

Contemporary Realistic Fiction

Bolognese, Don. ***A New Day.*** Delacorte, 1970. — 4–6

This is a contemporary retelling of the Nativity in which a child is born in a service station to migrant workers, Maria and José.

Byars, Betsy C. ***Midnight Fox.*** Illustrated by Ann Grifaloconi. Viking, 1968. — 4–6

Tommy is a nonathlete who has a long list of fears. He has an awesome and beautiful experience when he is sent to the farm for the summer.

Cleary, Beverly. ***Henry and Beezus.*** Illustrated by Louis Darling. Morrow, 1952. — 3–5

Henry Huggins and his dog Ribsy find themselves busily trying to raise money to buy a bicycle.

Cleary, Beverly. ***Ramona the Pest.*** Illustrated by Louis Darling. Morrow, 1968. — 3–5

Ramona becomes a "kindergarten dropout" despite her good intentions. Her uncontrollable curiosity is a contributing factor!

Cleaver, Vera, and Bill Cleaver. ***Lady Ellen Grae.*** Illustrated by Ellen Raskin. Harper, 1968. — 6–8

Eleven-year-old Ellen befriends a solitary but harmless old man. He confesses the story of his brutal parents and what he did to them. Ellen becomes aware of her responsibilities in the situation.

	Grade span	Culture

Cunningham, Julia. *Dorp Dead.* Illustrated by James Spanfeller. Pantheon, 1968. — **6–8**

This is the subtle horror story of Gilly Ground, who expresses his defiance of the world in the phrase "Dorp Dead."

DeJong, Meindert. *The Wheel on the School.* Illustrated by Maurice Sendak. Harper Junior Books, 1954. — **5–6**

The children of Shora, a Netherlands village, are determined to bring the storks back to their town.

Dunne, Mary Collins. *Reach Out, Ricardo.* Abelard-Schuman, 1971. — **4–8** **H**

The life of a fifteen-year-old Mexican American becomes increasingly complicated when his father joins the grape workers' strike.

Enright, Elizabeth. *Gone-Away Lake.* Harcourt, 1957. — **4–6**

Portia and Julian make marvelous discoveries in the woods around their summer home. They explore old houses and hear glorious stories of bygone times.

Enright, Elizabeth. *Saturdays.* Holt, 1941. — **4–6**

Four motherless children and their father devise a scheme for taking turns, on Saturdays, in spending their allowance on the pleasures and adventures in their hometown of New York City.

Farley, Walter. *The Black Stallion.* Illustrated by Keith Ward. Random House, 1941. — **3–5**

This is the story of Alec Ramsay's love for a magnificent wild horse. A strange understanding develops between the two as they share all sorts of dangers and adventures.

Fitzhugh, Louise. *Nobody's Family Is Going to Change.* Farrar, 1974. — **5–8**

Emma Sheridan, eleven years old, wants to be a lawyer. Her little brother Willie dreams of being a dancer. Their father wants Willie to be the lawyer and does not really care what Emma does.

George, Jean C. *My Side of the Mountain.* Dutton, 1959. — **4–8**

Sam Gribley does what many young people dream of doing. He spends a winter alone on a mountain in the Catskills.

Greene, Constance C. *A Girl Called Al.* Illustrated by Byron Barton. Viking, 1969. — **4–6**

A warm friendship develops between two girls who live in a city apartment house. One of the girls is Al, who is sort of fat and a nonconformist but very interesting.

Hale, Janet C. *The Owl's Song.* Doubleday, 1974. — **6–9** **I**

This is a sensitive portrayal of a young Indian boy's struggle to survive in a world that is determined to erase his identity. Billy White Hawk finds happiness in his artistic creations, but tensions and anger lead to an explosion with unexpected results.

	Grade span	Culture

Henry, Marguerite. *Brighty of the Grand Canyon.* Rand McNally, 1953. — **4-5**

A shaggy burro witnesses the destruction of his friend, an old man. Years later he vindicates his friend's death by helping to capture the murderer.

Henry, Marguerite. *Justin Morgan Had a Horse.* Illustrated by Wesley Dennis. Wilcox, 1945; Rand McNally, 1954. — **3-4**

This is the story of a common, ordinary little workhorse that labors hard all day and takes part in races and pulling contests at night. The horse turns out to be the father of a famous family of American horses.

Henry, Marguerite. *Misty of Chincoteague.* Illustrated by Wesley Dennis. Rand McNally, 1947. — **4-6**

This is a story of two freedom-loving ponies and of Paul and Maureen, who want to own them. Paul and Maureen manage to tame the wild mare and win final triumph on Pony-Penning Day.

Hillerman, Tony. *Dance Hall of the Dead.* Harper Junior Books, 1973. — **6-9** | **I**

In this suspenseful story a young Navajo is murdered by a manifestation of the Navajo Wolf (or werewolf). The murder is resolved by a Blue Policeman, whose investigation leads to local hippies, anthropologists, and the world of strange religious beliefs.

Konigsburg, E. L. *About the B'nai Bagels.* Atheneum, 1969. — **5-7**

Mark Setzer plays on the Little League team called the B'nai Bagels. With his mother as manager and brother as coach, he has many problems. In addition, he has to worry about his performance at his bar mitzvah.

Lampman, Evelyn S. *Go Up the Road.* Atheneum, 1972. — **4-8** | **H**

Yolanda Ruiz's family has to leave their New Mexican village each year to go north and harvest crops. Yolanda has to leave school early to join them. Finally, a visit to her aunt in Oregon opens Papa's eyes to the possibilities of a new life.

Lampman, Evelyn S. *The Potlatch Family.* Atheneum, 1976. — **6-9** | **I**

Looked down at by her classmates because of her darker skin and alcoholic father, a Chinook Indian girl gains a new outlook when her brother returns from Vietnam.

Mann, Peggy. *My Dad Lives in a Downtown Hotel.* Illustrated by Richard Cuffari. Avon, 1973; Doubleday, 1973. — **3-5**

A boy tries to adjust to his parents' separation. Thinking that the separation is his fault, Joey visits his father and tries to persuade him to come back.

McCloskey, Robert. *Homer Price.* Puffin, 1943, 1971. — **4-5**

These six preposterous tales are set in midwestern America. From the breathtaking suspense of Mystery Yarn to the extravagant affair of the Doughnuts, Homer Price has the world well under control.

Morey, Walt. *Gentle Ben.* Illustrated by John Schoenherr. Dutton, 1965. — **5-7**

Mark, thirteen, befriends a tame Alaskan brown bear that has been chained in a shed from the time it was a cub. The story is set in Alaska before it became a state.

	Grade span	Culture

Neville, Emily C. *It's Like This, Cat.* Illustrated by Emil Weiss. Harper Junior Books, 1963. — **6–8**

This is a tale of Dave's affection for a stray tomcat, his first shy friendship with a girl, and his growing understanding for his father as a person and not just a parent.

O'Dell, Scott. *The Black Pearl.* Dell, 1967; Houghton, 1967. — **4–6** | H

Sixteen-year-old Ramon dreams of someday becoming a partner with his father pearling the waters of Baja California. Possession of the giant "Pearl of Heaven" reshapes his life and gains him two enemies.

O'Dell, Scott. *Child of Fire.* Houghton, 1974. — **4–6** | H

A parole officer relates his efforts to keep the violence and heroics of two young Chicanos under control.

Paul, Paula G. *You Can Hear a Magpie Smile.* Elsevier/Nelson, 1980. — **4–6** | H

Lupe tries to help her friend, the local herb woman, when she learns a medical clinic is planned for her village in New Mexico.

Politi, Leo. *Three Stalks of Corn.* Scribner, 1976. — **K–2** | H

Angelica discovers the value of her heritage through legends taught by her grandmother, and she shares these "lessons" at school.

Raskin, Ellen. *The Westing Game.* Dutton, 1978. — **5–7**

The mysterious death of an eccentric millionaire brings together an unlikely assortment of heirs.

Robinson, Barbara. *The Best Christmas Pageant Ever.* Illustrated by Judith Gwyn Brown. Harper Junior Books, 1972. — **3–4**

The six mean Herdman kids lie, steal, smoke cigars, and then become involved in the community Christmas pageant.

Sachs, Marilyn. *Veronica Ganz.* Illustrated by Louis Glanzman. Doubleday, 1968. — **4–6**

Veronica is tormented by a new student, Peter Wedemeyer. If she does not defend herself, who will? Her strategies fail time after time, until she does something she has never done before and discovers that "the weapon" she had been searching for was one she had always possessed.

Snyder, Zilpha K. *The Egypt Game.* Illustrated by Alton Raible. Atheneum, 1967. — **5–6**

Six children of different ethnic backgrounds secretly play a game invented by a white girl and a black girl who are fascinated by their own imaginations and by ancient Egypt. The Egypt game helps solve one girl's personal problems and leads to the capture of a murderer.

Sobol, Donald J. *Encyclopedia Brown Sets the Pace.* Illustrated by Ib Ohlsson. Four Winds, 1982. — **4–5**

The reader tries to solve ten mysteries along with Encyclopedia Brown. The mysteries are largely solvable if the reader is sharp.

Tobias, Tobi. *The Quitting Deal.* Viking, 1975. — **3–5**

A mother and daughter agree to help one another stop their two bad habits: smoking and thumb-sucking.

	Grade span	Culture

Todd, Barbara K. *Juan Patricio.* Illustrated by Gloria Kamen. Putnam, 1972.

2-3 H

Everyone has a summer job in Santa Fe except Juan. He tries to help Mama, but he is too small. He decides to help his neighbor, but he only causes problems. Finally, after many disappointments, he finds a job that is just right for him.

Wrightson, Patricia. *A Racecourse for Andy.* Harcourt, 1968.

6-8

Sydney, Australia, is the setting for this story about "mentally retarded Andy (who) 'buys' the local racetrack from a bottlepicker. Convinced that he is the owner, no amount of logic can persuade Andy that he is not."

Historical Fiction

Bacon, Martha. *Sophia Scrooby Preserved.* Little, 1968.

6-8

An African chieftain's daughter is taken into slavery and grows up in New England with the Scrooby family. She is captured first by pirates and then by a voodoo queen. She becomes a companion to an English lady, and she performs on stage before being reunited with the Scrooby family.

Banks, Lynne Reid. *The Indian in the Cupboard* (General). Doubleday, 1980.

6-9 I

A nine-year-old boy receives an old medicine cupboard and a key for his birthday. He finds himself involved in an adventure when a small plastic Indian comes to life in the cupboard and befriends him.

Baylor, Byrd. *Hawk, I'm Your Brother* (Southwest). Scribner, 1976.

K-3 I

Ruby Sato catches a hawk that he later releases. He finds that he can still communicate with the hawk and is able to experience flying vicariously. When he gives the hawk its freedom, he finds new power and becomes the hawk's brother.

Bulla, Clyde R. *Riding the Pony Express.* Illustrated by Grace Paull. Crowell, 1948.

4-5

This is a western frontier adventure story that takes place at a Pony Express way station and involves three children: Dick, Katy, and Little Bear.

Coerr, Eleanor B. *Sadako and the Thousand Paper Cranes.* Putnam, 1977.

4-8 J

This is the true story of a Japanese girl who died of leukemia as a result of the Hiroshima atomic bomb. Sadako's effort to have faith in the legend of the Golden Crane is beautifully portrayed. A statue of Sadako can be found today in Hiroshima's Peace Park.

Craven, Margaret. *I Heard the Owl Call My Name* (Northwest). Doubleday, 1973.

7-9 I

In a powerful and sensitive story, a man discovers the fundamental truths of love and life, courage and dignity, when he is sent to live in a remote coastal village among the proud Indians of northwestern Canada prior to his early death.

	Grade span	Culture

The Girl Who Married a Ghost and Other Tales of the North American Indians. Edited by John Bierhorst. Four Winds, 1978. **[5–9] [I]**

Nine haunting stories of the North American Indians are presented. The edited book includes beautiful pictures and a brief summary of geographical and tribal information for each selection.

Goble, Paul, and Dorothy Goble. *Lone Bull's Horse Raid* (Plains). Bradbury Press, 1973. **[6–8] [I]**

This is the story of an Indian named Lone Bull. It tells of his first horse-stealing raid and the battle that followed. In the battle he stands before his people as a warrior.

Gray, Elizabeth Janet. *Adam of the Road.* Illustrated by Robert Lawson. Viking, 1942. **[5–7]**

A thirteenth-century minstrel boy searches through southeastern England for his father and dog.

Houston, Jeanne W., and James Houston. *Farewell to Manzanar.* Houghton, 1973. **[6–8] [J]**

This is a true story of one spirited Japanese-American family's attempt to survive the indignities of forced detention and of a native-born American child who discovered what it was like to grow up behind barbed wire in the United States.

Jones, Weynan. *Edge of Two Worlds.* Dial Books, 1968. **[6–8]**

Young Calvin Harper, the only survivor of an Indian attack on his wagon train, meets an old Cherokee from whom he gains wisdom and maturity and decides to continue his journey east to attend law school.

Kerr, Judith. *When Hitler Stole Pink Rabbit.* Coward, 1972. **[5–6]**

When Anna and her family flee Berlin, they struggle with new languages, customs, and schools. The family adjusts to temporary homes in Zurich and Paris and finds much to value in the new life.

Konigsburg, E. L. *A Proud Taste for Scarlet and Miniver.* Atheneum, 1973. **[7–8]**

Eleanor of Aquitaine and three of her contemporaries recall her life, including the power struggles, pomp, and pageantry of her twelfth-century world, from a perch in heaven.

McCunn, Ruthanne L. *Pie-Biter.* Design Enterprises, 1983. **[4–8] [C]**

Hoi comes from China to help build the railroad. His love for American pies helps him gain in size and strength. With the help of his friend, he uses a clever ruse that sets him on the path toward becoming a successful packer.

McSwigan, Marie. *Snow Treasure.* Illustrated by Mary Reardon. Dutton, 1942. **[3–5]**

This is a true story of how brave Norwegian boys and girls outwitted the Nazi invaders and rendered a great service to their country. The children carried blocks of gold out of Germany by fastening them to their sleds and coasting through the German camps.

PARENTS PLAY ROLES OF INESTIMABLE IMPORTANCE IN LAYING THE FOUNDATION FOR LEARNING TO READ.

	Grade span	Culture

O'Dell, Scott. *The King's Fifth.* Houghton, 1966. **4–6**

A young cartographer with Coronado recalls all that happened on the hazardous, inglorious journey he made with Captain Mendoza and five others to the Seven Cities of Cibola to find gold.

O'Dell, Scott. *Sing Down the Moon* (Navajo). Houghton, 1970. **6–9** I

This story is based on the conflict between Navajo Indians and white settlers during the Civil War period. It is told in the first person by a young Navajo girl who is kidnapped and enslaved by Spaniards, then rescued by her husband-to-be.

Rockwood, Joyce. *To Spoil the Sun* (Cherokee). Holt, 1976. **6–9** I

This is a fictionalized picture of Cherokee life in the southern Appalachians during the sixteenth century, shortly after the arrival of the first Europeans to the New World.

Sachs, Marilyn. *A Pocket Full of Seeds.* Doubleday. 1973. **5–6**

In the five years during which Nazi terror increasingly encroaches on her life, Nicole Nieman, a French Jew, grows from a smug little girl of eight to a resourceful teenager.

Saiki, Patsy Sumie. *Sachie: Daughter of Hawaii.* Kisaku, 1977. **4–6** J

The life and customs of a Japanese-American girl in Hawaii are described.

Sandoz, Mari. *The Horsecatcher* (Cheyenne). Westminster, 1957. **6–9** I

Young Elk, a Cheyenne youth, loves to catch and tame wild horses of the prairies. When he captures a beautiful white stallion, his people are attacked. Young Elk frees the horse to bring peace.

Sandoz, Mari. *The Story Catcher* (Sioux). Westminster, 1963. **6–9** I

Young Lance of the Oglala Sioux Indian tribe undergoes many winters of hardship, adventure, and sorrow before the people of Sun Shield village recognize him as Story Catcher and band historian. The story depicts the life of the Plains Indians as they cling to the old ways on the tragic eve of their end.

Santa Elena, Antonio E. *Mahinhin: A Tale of the Philippines.* Downey Place, 1984. **4–8** F

A twelve-year-old girl "comes of age" in a small Philippine town near Manila during the 1950s.

Sawyer, Ruth. *Roller Skates.* Viking, 1936. **5–7**

For one glorious school year, Lucinda's parents go to Europe, and she is free of her governess and the other duties of her privileged childhood. With a pair of skates and a bold, compassionate soul, Lucinda makes friends and has adventures in all parts of New York City.

Schweitzer, Byrd Baylor. *One Small Blue Bead* (Southwest). Macmillan, 1965. **K–3** I

A bead lies in the desert sand of Arizona. Once it was treasured by a boy who lived in prehistoric times. In simple rhyming text this book tells how the boy met a boy from a distant tribe and was given the bead.

	Grade span	Culture

Uchida, Yoshiko. *A Jar of Dreams; The Best Bad Thing;* and *The Happiest Ending* (Trilogy). Atheneum, 1981, 1983, 1985.
[4–8] [J]

These three books tell the story of a Japanese-American girl, Rinko, and her family living in Berkeley during the depression. Through day-to-day events, we see Rinko deal with racial prejudice and grow to accept her own racial and cultural identity.

Wilder, Laura Ingalls. *Little House on the Prairie.* Illustrated by Garth Williams. Harper Junior Books, 1953.
[4–8]

In this book about the pioneer Ingalls family, Ma, Pa, and the girls move from the Wisconsin woods to the wild Kansas prairie. It gives a daily account of how they establish a homestead where before only tall grasses and wild animals lived.

Yep, Laurence. *Dragonwings.* Harper Junior Books, 1975.
[5–6] [C]

In 1903 Moonshadow travels from a remote village in China to California to join his father whom he has never seen. Despite tremendous difficulties and disasters, father and son struggle to live in San Francisco while always working toward their dream of creating a dragon-like flying machine.

Nonfiction—Information

Arnold, Caroline. *Five Nests.* Illustrated by Ruth Sanderson. Dutton, 1980.
[2–4]

All birds lay eggs, and then the eggs hatch. Some birds in this book may live near you, so you can watch them. Then you can see who takes care of the babies.

Barton, Byron. *Airport.* Harper Junior Books, 1982.
[1–3]

This book shows people coming to the airport in cars, buses, and taxis and captures the activities and magic of an airport.

Baylor, Byrd. *When Clay Sings* (Southwest). Scribner, 1972.
[K–5] [I]

The author and artist, in putting together some of the pieces of prehistoric Indian pottery that can be found in the desert hillsides of the West, have created a picture of the past that depicts the Indian way of life in an earlier time.

Behrens, June. *Gung hay fat choy: Happy New Year.* Children's Press, 1982.
[K–3] [C]

Illustrated with colored photographs, this book documents the celebration of the Chinese New Year by Chinese Americans.

The Butterfly Cycle. Photographs by John Cooke. Putnam, 1977.
[3–4]

The four stages in the life cycle of a butterfly are seen in close-up color photographs. The brief captions complete the story.

Clark, Ann Nolan. *Along Sandy Trails* (Papago). Viking, 1969.
[K–3] [I]

A Papago Indian grandmother and young granddaughter walk together in the Arizona desert. They share the beauty and variety of nature through poetic words and magnificent color photographs.

	Grade span	Culture

Cobb, Vicki, and Kathy Darling. ***Bet You Can't! Science Impossibilities to Fool You.*** Illustrated by Martha Weston. Lothrop, 1980. **2–4**

This is an entertaining and enticing introduction to basic scientific principles. The authors use tricks that have natural causes at work.

Davis, Daniel S. ***Behind Barbed Wire: The Imprisonment of Japanese Americans During World War II.*** Dutton, 1982. **4–6** **J**

This book describes the lives of 120,000 Japanese Americans who lived in "relocation" camps during World War II.

DePaola, Tomie. ***The Cloud Book.*** Holiday House, 1975. **K–3**

Clouds tell us about coming changes in the weather. The book introduces the ten most common clouds and some ancient myths inspired by clouds.

DePaola, Tomie. ***The Popcorn Book.*** Holiday House, 1978. **K–3**

This book contains a variety of facts about popcorn and two recipes for cooking it. The book is a blend of information and humor.

Filstrup, Chris, and Janie Filstrup. ***Beadazzled.*** Illustrated by Loren Bloom. Frederick Warne, 1982. **K–3**

This carefully researched book explores the many ways that beads have been used in the past and are being used today. Special craft projects are described at the end of the book.

Fitch, Lanne, and Bob Fitch. ***Soy Chicano: I Am Mexican-American.*** Creative Educational Society, 1970. **3–6** **H**

The daily experiences of a thirteen-year-old Mexican-American girl in a small agricultural town in California are described.

Goor, Ron, and Nancy Goor. ***Shadows: Here, There, and Everywhere.*** Harper Junior Books, 1981. **K–3**

The authors use striking photographs to explain how shadows are formed, why they change, and why they are important to us.

Graham, Ada, and Frank Graham. ***The Changing Desert.*** Illustrated by Robert B. Shetterly. Sierra Club Books/Scribner, 1981. **3–5**

The American desert is being changed and destroyed by human visitors. People from all walks of life are trying to save the rare plants and animals of the Southwest. This book explores the mysteries and problems of the desert.

Greenfeld, Howard. ***Bar Mitzvah.*** Illustrated by Elaine Grove. Holt, 1981. **6–8**

This book explains the history and significance of the bar mitzvah ceremony for boys and the newer bat mitzvah for girls and tells what the ceremonies mean in the life of a Jew.

Hess, Lilo. ***The Amazing Earthworm.*** Scribner, 1979. **1–3**

Using text and photographs, the author explores the life, habitat, and practical uses of earthworms, adding simple experiments that children can perform.

	Grade span	Culture

Hewett, Joan. *Watching Them Grow.* Photographs by Richard Hewett. Little, 1979. — **1–4**

The inner workings of a zoo nursery are revealed in diary form. The author describes the care and training that young animals receive before being housed with the adults.

Kalb, Jonah, and Laura Kalb. *The Easy Ice Skating Book.* Illustrated by Sandy Kossin. Houghton, 1981. — **2–4**

The authors make ice skating easy as they describe everything the beginning skater needs to know for fun and success in the first year on the ice.

Koebner, Linda. *From Cage to Freedom: A New Beginning for Laboratory Chimpanzees.* Dutton, 1981. — **3–5**

The author relates her experiences in returning a group of laboratory chimpanzees to freedom in an animal preserve in Florida.

Kohn, Bernice. *Talking Leaves: The Story of Sequoyah.* Hawthorn, 1969. — **4–7** — I

This is the biography of the Cherokee Indian, Sequoyah, who developed the first written Indian alphabet.

Mannetti, William. *Dinosaurs in Your Backyard.* Atheneum, 1982. — **3–5**

Scientists have come up with some new theories about dinosaurs, their nature, and their physiology. The giant animals, once assuredly reptilian, are now thought to have been warm-blooded. This book takes a new look at what scientists are learning about dinosaurs

Math, Irwin. *Morse, Marconi and You: Understanding and Building Telegraph, Telephone and Radio Sets.* Scribner, 1979. — **3–6**

In this clear step-by-step guide, the author shows how the reader can build telegraph, telephone, and radio sets and demonstrates why they work.

McClung, Robert M. *America's Endangered Birds: Programs and People Working to Save Them.* Illustrated by George Founds. Morrow, 1979. — **5–6**

The author examines the plight of six endangered birds, including the bald eagle and California condor, and discusses the latest research on their reproduction.

McDearmon, Kay. *Foxes.* Dodd, 1981. — **K–3**

The author examines the physical characteristics, eating habits, family life, and enemies of several kinds of foxes.

McDearmon, Kay. *Rocky Mountain Bighorns.* Photographs by Valerius Geist. Dodd, 1980. — **2–5**

The author introduces the Rocky Mountain Bighorn sheep and discusses their physical characteristics, habitat, behavior, care of the young, natural enemies, and need for protection.

McGaw, Jessie B. *Chief Red Horse Tells About Custer.* Lodestar Books, 1981. — **6–9** — I

This brief book, which includes a story, a code book, and a bit of American history, presents a fascinating account by an eyewitness of "Custer's Last Stand." Five years after the Battle of Little Bighorn, a Sioux warrior told his version of events in sign language while an army surgeon took down the tale in diagrams.

	Grade span	Culture

Schaaf, Peter. *An Apartment House Close Up.* Four Winds/ Macmillan, 1980. — **4-6**

The author presents a virtually wordless photographic study of the outside and interior of an apartment house.

Scott, Jack Denton. *Moose.* Photographs by Ozzie Sweet. Putnam, 1981. — **2-4**

The author describes the moose, that northern creature that is the "world's largest living deer."

Selsam, Millicent E. *How to Be a Nature Detective.* Illustrated by Ezra Jack Keats. Harper Junior Books, 1963. — **4-6**

The reader learns how to identify and interpret animal tracks and clues.

Selsam, Millicent E. *The Plants We Eat.* Photographs by Jerome Wexler. Morrow, 1981. — **1-3**

The author discusses the development of the most common food plants and their changing uses. Simple directions for growing some of the plants at home are included.

Selsam, Millicent E. *Popcorn.* Photographs by Jerome Wexler. Morrow, 1976. — **K-3**

The growth cycle of popcorn is described.

Selsam, Millicent E., and Jerome Wexler. *The Amazing Dandelion.* Morrow, 1977. — **1-3**

The author discusses the life cycle of the dandelion, an extremely hearty plant with often-overlooked nutritional value.

Simon, Seymour. *Animal Fact: Animal Fable.* Illustrated by Diane DeGroat. Crown, 1979. — **3-6**

In this account of some common beliefs about animals, the author asks the reader to guess whether each belief is fact or fable before turning the page to find the answer.

Simon, Seymour. *The Long Journey from Space.* Crown, 1982. — **3-6**

The author describes what comets and meteors are, how we came to know about them, what their special characteristics are, and what some of the more famous of them look like.

Simon, Seymour. *The Secret Clocks: Time Senses of Living Things.* Illustrated by Jan Brett. Viking, 1979. — **4-5**

The author explains the occurrence of biological clocks that, for example, "tell" birds when and where to migrate and plants, when to unfurl their leaves.

Swinburne, Irene, and Lawrence Swinburne. *Behind the Sealed Door: The Discovery of the Tomb and Treasures of Tutankhamen.* Sniffen Court Books, 1977 (distributed by Atheneum). — **4-6**

The author describes the work of the archaeologists, the magnificent treasures they found, and the life of Tutankhamen. The book includes a mylar insert showing the coffins and mummy of Tutankhamen.

	Grade span	Culture

Tresselt, Alvin. *White Snow, Bright Snow.* Illustrated by Roger Duvoisin. Lothrop, 1947. — **1-3**

The delight and wonder of a winter snowfall are described.

Walker, Barbara M. *The Little House Cookbook: Frontier Foods from Laura Ingalls Wilder's Classic Stories.* Illustrated by Garth Williams. Harper Junior Books, 1979. — **4-6**

The book includes recipes that are mentioned in the *Little House* books by Laura Ingalls Wilder.

Weber, William J. *Care of Uncommon Pets.* Holt, 1979. — **3-5**

This book is a summary of the proper way to provide food and shelter for unusual household pets. It is written in a narrative style and usually from the author's own experience. Each chapter is devoted to a different animal, some of which are rabbits, hamsters, chickens, frogs, turtles, and snakes.

Weiss, Harvey. *Hammer and Saw.* Harper Junior Books, 1981. — **3-6**

This is a good introduction to the basics of woodworking. The book includes simple projects (for example, checkerboard, weather vane, and chest).

Wolf, Bernard. *In This Proud Land: The Story of a Mexican-American Family.* Lippincott, 1978. — **4-8** | **H**

This book is a collection of black-and-white photographs and short narrations of an exceptionally successful, though poor, Mexican-American family. Success is determined by the personal goals for college educations and the unselfish family relationships between the children and adults.

Nonfiction—Biography

Aaseng, Nathan. *Winners Never Quit.* Lerner, 1980. — **3-6**

Careers of athletes with some kind of disability are discussed. It is fast moving, with colorful descriptions of athletic competitions. The photographs are black and white.

Aldis, Dorothy. *Nothing Is Impossible: The Story of Beatrix Potter.* Illustrated by Richard Cuffari. Atheneum, 1969. — **3-6**

This is a biography of the author-illustrator who created Peter Rabbit. It conveys her enchantment with nature and country life.

Brenner, Barbara. *On the Frontier with Mr. Audubon.* Coward, 1977. — **4-6**

This is the fictionalized diary of a thirteen-year-old boy who travels downriver on a flatboat in 1820 with John James Audubon, the famous naturalist and artist.

Brenner, Barbara. *A Snake-Lover's Diary.* Young Scott Books, 1970. — **4-6**

This informative and entertaining book describes ways of catching and caring for reptiles and relates adventures involving and problems encountered with these animals both in the wild and as pets.

MAKE FREE STUDENT RESPONSE A PART OF EACH CLASSROOM READING LESSON.

	Grade span	Culture

Ceserani, Gian P. *Christopher Columbus.* Illustrated by Piero Ventura. Random, 1979. `3–5`

This is the story of the man who, while exploring the unknown world, discovered America.

Ceserani, Gian P. *Marco Polo.* Illustrated by Piero Ventura. Putnam, 1982. `4–6`

The author relates the adventures of the eighteenth-century merchant from Venice who wrote a famous account of his Asian travels and his life at the court of Kublai Khan.

Demuth, Patricia. *Joel: Growing Up a Farm Man.* Dodd, Mead, 1982. `3–5`

This book focuses on a thirteen-year-old boy who works on his family's farm caring for livestock, harvesting hay, and preparing to manage the farm himself one day.

De Pauw, Linda G. *Founding Mothers: Women of America in the Revolutionary Era.* Houghton, 1975. `3–5`

The roles of women who lived during the Revolutionary era are presented from a contemporary feminist perspective. The book includes tales of women soldiers, spies, organizers, couriers, and political activists.

De Pauw, Linda G. *Seafaring Women.* Houghton, 1982. `3–6`

This is a book about the lives of women on the seas from ancient times to the present, including women mariners in mythology and folklore, women pirates, women on whaling and trading ships, and contemporary women in the military services at sea.

Facklam, Margery. *Wild Animals, Gentle Women.* Harcourt, 1978. `4–6`

This is a readable and entertaining description of the experiences of 11 women who studied animal behavior.

Forbes, Esther. *America's Paul Revere.* Houghton, 1946. `2–4`

The life of one of America's foremost patriots and craftsmen is told in flowing prose and through striking color and black-and-white illustrations by Lynd Ward.

Goodman, Saul. *Baryshnikov: A Most Spectacular Dancer.* Harvey House, 1979. `4–6`

The author traces the artistic and professional growth of the ballet superstar and briefly comments on Baryshnikov as a person.

Inouye, Daniel K., with Lawrence Elliott. *Journey to Washington.* Prentice-Hall, 1967. `6–8` `J`

This is an autobiography of the first Japanese American to be elected to Congress. Senator Inouye's strong Americanism is based on faith in democracy.

Kroeber, Theodora. *Ishi, Last of His Tribe* (Yahi, California). Houghton/Parnassus Press, 1964. `6–9` `I`

This is a story of the last survivor of the Yahi Indian tribe. He makes a transition from life in a Stone Age culture to modern civilization.

	Grade span	Culture

Lipsyte, Robert. *Free to Be Muhammad Ali.* Harper Junior Books, 1978. — 4-6, B

This book covers the life of the boxer Muhammad Ali through childhood, boxing triumphs, exile from boxing, and comeback.

Place, Marian T. *Marcus and Narcissa Whitman: Oregon Pioneers.* Garrard, 1967. — 4-6

A courageous couple travels to the West, hoping to bring Christianity and "civilization" to the Indians in Oregon.

Santrey, Laurence. *Young Frederick Douglass: Fight for Freedom.* Troll Associates, 1983. — 4-6, B

Frederick Douglass, a black man, became a champion of his people.

Syme, Ronald. *Geronimo: The Fighting Apache* (Apache). Morrow, 1975. — 4-6, I

This biography covers Geronimo's life from youth to death. It emphasizes his battles against the "White Eyes."

Takashima, Shizuye. *A Child in Prison Camp.* Tundra Books, 1971. — 4-6, J

A Japanese-Canadian girl spends three years in an internment camp during World War II as a possible "security risk."

Tobias, Tobi. *Maria Tallchief.* Illustrated by Michael Hapshire. Crowell, 1970. — 4-6, I

Maria's father was Osage, her mother Scotch-Irish. She had dancing and piano lessons early in life. Later she became a famous ballet dancer with the Ballet Russe Company. The writing is simple and factual with ethnic and cultural appeal.

Vinke, Herman. *The Short Life of Sophie Scholl.* Translated from the German. Harper, 1984. — 3-5

A young German girl demonstrates courage in the resistance movement during the Nazi era.

Wibberley, Leonard. *A Dawn in the Trees: The Thomas Jefferson Years, 1776—1789.* Ariel Books, 1964. — 4-6

This book starts with the debate concerning the Declaration of Independence, which Jefferson alone had first written. It ends with his final triumph over despair at his wife's death, when he at last begins to see "a dawn in the trees."

Wibberly, Leonard. *Young Man from the Piedmont: The Youth of Thomas Jefferson.* Ariel Books, 1963. — 4-6

The author gives an account of the early life of Jefferson, 1743—1770s. It begins with his birth in Virginia and closes when Mr. Jefferson dips his pen in the inkhorn and begins to write, "When in the . . . ."

Woods, Harold, and Geraldine Woods. *Bill Cosby: Making America Laugh and Learn.* Dillon Press, 1983. — 2-5, B

This is the story of Bill Cosby, a black comedian and educator who is also known as the creator of Fat Albert, Weird Harold, and other assorted characters from his childhood.

MATERIALS FOR STUDENTS IN GRADES SEVEN AND EIGHT

Young people in the seventh and eighth grades have reading tastes that lead forward and backward—forward to the world of the young adults that they are becoming and backward to the time of childhood that they are leaving. Because many students leave school early, it is also the last time for most of these readers that academic assignments will permit opportunities to read widely. Therefore, a list of books must provide these readers with wide choices to examine the future and to relive or rethink their past.

The lists of selected entries are representative rather than comprehensive. The books have been chosen to address the following criteria: (1) good authors; (2) cultural diversity; (3) differing ability levels; and (4) the model curriculum standards for kindergarten through grade eight.

The entries are divided into categories, and a matrix is provided to give information to users of the lists. The categories are Adventure, Biography and Autobiography, Personal Experience, Classics, Contemporary Realism, Folk Literature and Folk Heroes, Historical Fiction, Mystery, Mythology, Science Fiction and Fantasy, Short Stories, and Plays.

The columns of the matrix will indicate the type of entry, i.e., core (C), extended (E), or recreational/motivational (R) (see definitions in the introduction to the document), and culture. The literary contributions of specific ethnic or cultural groups are identified by one of the following symbols:

B — Black   I — American Indian
C — Chinese   J — Japanese
F — Filipino   K — Korean
H — Hispanic   V — Vietnamese

	Type of entry	Culture

Adventure

Bell, Clare. *Ratha's Creature.* Atheneum, 1983.

In this story, which is set millions of years ago, the characters are animals that exhibit almost-human tendencies and emotions. Ratha is exiled from her (cat) clan and joins the neighboring enemy camp in attacking her former comrades. Before the conclusion, Ratha has gained knowledge of herself and her world.

> **C**

Buck, Pearl S. *The Big Wave.* John Day Company, 1947.

Two Japanese boys, Kino and Jiya, are only friends until the day a tidal wave sweeps away Jiya's family. Kino's family helps Jiya through his grief, and the boys grow up as brothers. The tale offers insights into Japanese culture and attitudes toward life, love, and death.

> **R** **J**

Burnford, Sheila. *The Incredible Journey.* Little, 1961.

A young Labrador retriever, an old bullterrier, and a Siamese cat trek through the Canadian wilderness and share the hazards of the journey. Each resists the human beings who try to prevent them from reaching their former home.

> **R**

George, Jean Craighead. *Julie of the Wolves.* Harper Junior Books, 1972.

Lost in the Alaskan wilderness, thirteen-year-old Miyax (Julie in English), an Eskimo girl, is gradually accepted by a pack of Arctic wolves that she comes to love. The novel is rich in descriptions of Eskimo customs and scenes of the wild tundra.

> **C**

Marshall, James Vance. *Walkabout.* William Morrow, 1971.

Two white children, Mary and Peter, sole survivors of a plane crash, meet a young Australian aborigine who is on his first walkabout. The bush boy, although resigned to death, resolves to lead the pair to safety. The book explores the belief in death by autosuggestion. Two very different cultures, the primitive and modern, are contrasted.

> **R**

Biography and Autobiography

Brooks, Polly Schoyer. *Queen Eleanor: Independent Spirit of the Medieval World.* Harper Junior Books, 1983.

This biography of Eleanor of Aquitaine contains valuable information on historic events and personages but keeps the spotlight on Eleanor. As queen of France, wife of Louis VII, and later queen of England, wife of Henry II, Eleanor proved herself a strong political negotiator as well as a person revered for cultivating the arts.

> **R**

George, Jean Craighead. *Cry of the Crow.* Harper Junior Books, 1980.

While caring for a baby crow, Mandy begins to look at her family and herself in a different light.

> **R** **I**

Harris, Jacqueline L. *Martin Luther King, Jr.* Watts, 1983.

Despite the shortage of personal and human insights into Martin Luther King, Jr., this is a well-documented, clearly written overview of the historic achievements of the civil rights movement and Dr. King.

> **C** **B**

	Type of entry	Culture

Keller, Helen Adams. *The Story of My Life.* Doubleday, 1903. — C

Left blind and deaf by a childhood illness, Helen Keller writes of her early life and education in Part One. Part Two is a collection of her letters written to friends. Part Three's material is drawn mainly from information, records, and letters provided by Helen's beloved teacher, Anne Sullivan.

O'Dell, Scott. *The Road to Damietta.* Houghton, 1985. — E

A woman of Assisi watches as Francis Bernardone turns from a life of privilege, takes vows of poverty, and devotes himself to serving God. This is an entirely new perspective on Saint Francis of Assisi.

Personal Experience

Brown, Marion, and Ruth Crone. *Silent Storm.* Abingdon Press, 1963; E. M. Hale, 1966. — R

This story of Anne Sullivan Macy relates the experiences of her many teaching years with Helen Keller, giving many insights into the personal side of Macy and the handicaps she overcame in bringing Helen out of her darkness.

Durrell, Gerald. *My Family and Other Animals.* Penguin Books, 1957, 1977. — R

As a boy, the author, a British zoologist, spent five years with his family on the island of Corfu. The friendly islanders gave him strange and wonderful animals for his collection. Interspersed with descriptions of the island and its wildlife are amusing accounts of the exploits of the Durrell family.

Frank, Anne. *The Diary of a Young Girl.* Doubleday, 1952. — E

Two Jewish families went into hiding in the abandoned half of a warehouse in Amsterdam during the Nazi occupation. Anne, the thirteen-year-old, recorded what she saw and felt about the relationships of eight people living under the strain of hunger, of crowded housing, and of fear of discovery and death. This is a moving account of the universal emotions of an adolescent.

Fritz, Jean. *Homesick: My Own Story.* Putnam, 1982. — E

This is a somewhat fictionalized account of the author's childhood in China. She writes of her days at the British school; of her amah; of the holidays shared with her friend, Andrea; of the burden of always having to "be good"; of the worry over the threatening war; and of the fears and loyalties of a young girl.

Hall, Lynn. *Just One Friend.* Scribner, 1985. — C

Just as sixteen-year-old learning-disabled Doreen is about to be mainstreamed into a regular school, the loss of her best friend to another girl drives her to a desperate act. Readers of this novel will gain new understanding of the world of the outsider.

Hamilton, Virginia. *Junius Over Far.* Harper Junior Books, 1985. — E — B

Three generations of strong black men, Jackabo the "wandering king," his successful but alienated son Damius, and the maturing, loving grandson Junius, are portrayed in this story set in the Caribbean.

〜〜〜〜〜〜

WELL-WRITTEN MATERIALS WILL NOT DO THE JOB ALONE. TEACHERS MUST INSTRUCT STUDENTS IN STRATEGIES FOR EXTRACTING AND ORGANIZING CRITICAL INFORMATION FROM TEXT.

	Type of entry	Culture
Herriot, James. ***All Creatures Great and Small.*** St. Martin's Press, 1972.	R	

In this warm, graphic account, the author tells of his life as a young veterinarian in Yorkshire, England, during the 1930s.

Kennedy, John F. ***Profiles in Courage.*** Harper Junior Books, 1964.	R	

This collection of profiles of Americans who took courageous stands at crucial moments in public life includes John Quincy Adams, Daniel Webster, Thomas Hart Benton, Sam Houston, Edmund G. Ross, Lucius Q. C. Lamar, George Norris, Robert A. Taft, and others.

Lipsyte, Robert. ***Free to Be Muhammad Ali.*** Harper Junior Books, 1978.	R	B

The text covers events in the life of Muhammad Ali from his boyhood through most of his trials and triumphs. The author highlights the champion's extraordinary career and charisma, but does not neglect to mention his human failings and the contradictions in Ali's character that make him one of the most controversial public figures of his time.

Mowat, Farley. ***The Dog Who Wouldn't Be.*** Little, 1977; Bantam, 1981.	R	

This humorous book is about a precocious canine that refused to be a dog. The dog's adventures are fun-loving extraordinary exploits.

Peck, Robert N. ***Soup on Ice.*** Knopf, 1985.	C	

Robert and his friend Soup engineer an incredible, exciting appearance of Santa in their small depression-era town in Vermont.

Petry, Ann. ***Harriet Tubman: Conductor of the Underground Railway.*** Harper Junior Books, 1955; Archway, 1971.	E	B

This is the story of a courageous black woman who, as a slave on a Maryland plantation, has dreams of freedom. Through her dreams and determination, she leads many slaves to freedom.

Sandburg, Carl. ***Abe Lincoln Grows Up.*** Harcourt, 1928, 1975.	C	

This adaptation of *Abraham Lincoln: The Prairie Years* deals with his early years up to age nineteen when he leaves home for New Salem, Illinois.

Yates, Elizabeth. ***Amos Fortune, Free Man.*** E. P. Dutton, 1950, 1967.	R	B

This is the biography of Amos, a black slave, from his capture in Africa to his life in America. Amos is purchased by a Quaker weaver, whose kindness and teachings influence the course of Amos's life.

Classics

Alcott, Louisa May. ***Little Women.*** Macmillan, 1986.	C	

The author tells the story of the four March sisters who lived in Civil War days. In their growing-up years, the sisters' adventures are affected by Jo, the fun-loving, rather impulsive sister.

Andersen, Hans Christian. ***The Snow Queen.*** Grosset and Dunlap, 1963; Penguin, 1982.	C	

This is a tale of seven stories based on the first story of an evil, distorting mirror. When it shatters, it causes an effect on all who are struck by it. The story caused by this effect is told by a young boy and girl.

	Type of entry	Culture

Barrie, James M. *Peter Pan*. Random House, 1983; Bantam, 1985. C

The early adventures of Peter Pan, a little boy who never grew up, is retold for young readers.

The Bible (selections). C

The Holy Bible contains the Old and New Testaments translated from the original tongues.

Defoe, Daniel. *Robinson Crusoe*. Grosset and Dunlap, 1963. C

A shipwreck's lone survivor is challenged to stay alive. Adventurous incidents in his everyday life lead to his discovery of other island inhabitants.

Dumas, Alexandre. *Count of Monte Cristo*. Bantam, 1976. C

Sentenced to life in prison for a crime that he did not commit, the hero escapes with an overwhelming determination to get revenge on his enemies.

Kroeber, Theodora. *Ishi, Last of His Tribe*. Bantam, 1976. C I

This is the true account of the lone survivor of the Yahi Indians of California, decimated by invading white settlers.

Lamb, Charles, and Mary Lamb. *Tales from Shakespeare*. Crowell, 1942. C

This is a retelling of 20 of Shakespeare's plays. The authors wrote the book as an introduction to the plays in story-form prose with dialogue and original language whenever possible.

London, Jack. *Call of the Wild*. Macmillan, 1956; Bantam, 1969. C

Buck, a mistreated sled dog, breaks free from his master and roams the Alaskan wilderness.

Miles, Bernard. *Favorite Tales from Shakespeare*. Rand McNally, 1984. C

The author presents five of Shakespeare's plays: *Macbeth, Midsummer Night's Dream, Romeo and Juliet, Twelfth Night,* and *Hamlet.* Well-done illustrations accompany the narratives.

Nye, Robert. *Beowulf: A New Telling*. Hill and Wang, 1968. C

A favorite theme of ancient legend is retold. The author emphasizes the triumph of good over evil. Beowulf, after a series of exciting experiences, overcomes and destroys Grendel, a monster.

Pyle, Howard. *Men of Iron*. Adapted by William Kottmeyer. McGraw-Hill, 1945; Airmont, 1975. C

In this story of pageantry, chivalry, and pomp, young Myles Falsworth vindicates his father and wins favor with King Henry IV.

Steinbeck, John. *The Red Pony*. Viking, 1945, 1959. C

This is a story of a young boy and his relationships with his sorrel colt, his father, and his friends. It is set in sunny California.

Stevenson, Robert Louis. *Kidnapped*. Grosset and Dunlap, 1948; Bantam, 1982. C

This well-known story tells of an adventure filled with shipwreck, hazards, and intrigue.

	Type of entry	Culture

Sutcliff, Rosemary. *The Sword and the Circle.* Dutton, 1981. **C**

The author recounts the quests, adventures, jousts, and loves of the Knights of the Round Table as well as what happened to King Arthur himself.

Tolkien, J. R. R. *The Hobbit.* Houghton, 1984. **C**

In this land of magic inhabited by dwarfs, elves, goblins, dragons, and humans, Bilbo Boggins, the hobbit, encounters many adventures when he is persuaded to join a band of dwarfs on an expedition to recover stolen treasure hidden by a thieving dragon in the depths of the lonely mountain.

Twain, Mark. *The Prince and the Pauper.* Bantam, 1982. **C**

By a strange accident, the boy king, Edward VI, becomes a poor boy and the poor boy becomes king. Exciting adventures bring out the pluckiness of the street waif, the manly courage of the nobly born, and the humanity of both.

Verne, Jules. *Around the World in Eighty Days.* Dodd, 1979; Airmont, 1964. **C**

The hero, Phileas Fogg, an Englishman, undertakes his hasty world tour as the result of a bet made at his London club. He and his French valet set out that very night and, by superhuman effort, succeed in making the circle of the globe ten minutes before the time agreed on 80 days later.

Wells, H. G. *War of the Worlds.* Putnam, 1978. **C**

Highly advanced Martians invade England and, with their command of superior weapons, overpower and prey on the English people.

Contemporary Realism

Bennett, Jack. *Voyage of the Lucky Dragon.* Prentice-Hall, 1981. **C**

Recent refugees during the Vietnam War display courage and find the meaning of freedom.

Brooks, Bruce. *The Moves Make the Man.* Harper Junior Books, 1984. **C** **B**

This novel, set in the black culture, is about a fatherless basketball player and his relationships at school.

Byars, Betsy C. *Summer of the Swans.* Viking, 1970. **R**

This is the story of sibling understanding. Her brother's retardation causes the sister to come to terms with herself and the world.

Cleaver, Vera, and Bill Cleaver. *Where the Lilies Bloom.* Lippincott, 1969. **R**

An Appalachian family learns resourcefulness when the father dies. The children accept responsibilities as they keep their promises to maintain a family.

Cunningham, Julia. *Dorp Dead.* Avon, 1974. **R**

Gilly, who expresses his defiance of the world in the phrase "Dorp Dead," is placed in a foster home. He comes to realize that the cage that is being built is meant for him.

	Type of entry	Culture

Greenfield, Eloise. *Sister.* Crowell, 1974. **R**

The search for identity after the death of a father is the source of motivation in this novel for adolescents.

Hall, Lynn. *Danza!* Scribner, 1981. **R**

A love for animals helps the protagonist accept responsibility and develop respect for grandparents by identifying with adults.

Hinton, Susie E. *The Outsiders.* Viking, 1967. **R**

A story of the conflicts in teenage life forms the theme of a moving novel involving social class and peer relations. The author wrote this when she herself was a teenager.

Levoy, Myron. *Alan and Naomie.* Harper Junior Books, 1977. **R**

An adolescent's escape from reality raises problems of peer pressures as the characters come to grips with questions of values, friendship, and prejudice.

Myers, Walter D. *Fast Sam, Cool Clyde, and Stuff.* Viking, 1975. **R B**

When Stuff moves to One Hundred Sixteenth Street in Harlem, his first problem is appearing extra cool so he can make new friends. He soon meets Sam and Clyde, and the three share sad times, adventures, and friendship. In their adventures, some poignant, some comic, Stuff and friends feel very close to each other.

Paterson, Katherine. *Jacob Have I Loved.* Harper Junior Books, 1980; Avon, 1981. **R**

Feeling deprived all her life of schooling, friends, mother, and even her name by her spoiled twin sister Carolina, Louise finally begins to find her identity.

Voigt, Cynthia. *Dicey's Song.* Atheneum, 1983. **E**

In this sequel to the novel *Homecoming,* the four abandoned Tillerman children are settled in with their grandmother. Thirteen-year-old Dicey, ever responsible for her three younger siblings, begins to build new ties and deal with old problems.

Wartski, Maureen C. *Boat to Nowhere.* Westminster Press, 1980. **R V**

Government representatives order Thay Van Chi and his grandchildren, Loc and Mai, to leave their peaceful Vietnam village. The three are saved by Kien, a tough city orphan. Kien has a small fishing vessel hidden. They set out for Thailand but are rebuffed when they arrive. After many adventures and the loss of Thay Van Chi, they are rescued by Americans.

Yep, Laurence. *Child of the Owl.* Harper Junior Books, 1977. **R C**

The story is set in San Francisco's Chinatown in the early 1960s. Casey, a young Chinese girl whose father is a compulsive gambler, must live for a time with her grandmother, Paw Paw, whom she has never seen. Casey has never thought of herself as Chinese, but life in Chinatown forces her to decide who she really is.

	Type of entry	Culture

Folk Literature and Folk Heroes

Bowman, James C. *Pecos Bill.* Albert Whitman, 1964.

    The author describes the exploits of the American folk hero, Pecos Bill, who was the greatest cowboy of them all.

R

Chase, Richard. *The Jack Tales.* Houghton, 1943.

    These Anglo-American folktales about the folk hero Jack and his brothers Will and Tom are told in the dialect and style of the mountain country of North Carolina. The tales are rich in the humor and earthiness of the mountain country. Some of the tales probably were brought to the area by the early English settlers.

R

Darling, Kathy. *Pecos Bill Finds a Horse.* Garrard, 1979.

    Pecos Bill, searching for something to ride, tries out a wildcat and a bear before settling on a spirited mustang.

R

Hamilton, Virginia. *The People Could Fly.* Knopf, 1985.

    These Afro-American folktales of animals, fantasy, the supernatural, and the desire for freedom, born of the sorrow of the slaves but passed on with hope, are excellent for reading aloud.

C **B**

Historical Fiction

Alter, Judith M. *Luke and the Van Zandt County War.* Texas Christian University Press, 1984.

    A fourteen-year-old girl relates how Van Zandt County withdrew from Texas after the Civil War.

R

Butterworth, Emma M. *As the Waltz Was Ending.* Four Winds, 1982.

    This is an autobiographical account of a young girl whose ballet career with the Vienna State Opera was interrupted by the invasion of the Nazis and who later had to fight for her life during the Russian occupation.

R

Collier, James L., and Christopher Collier. *My Brother Sam Is Dead.* Four Winds, 1974.

    This historical fiction novel recounts the tragedy that strikes the Meeker family during the Revolution when one son joins the rebel forces while the rest of the family tries to remain neutral in a divided town.

C

Greene, Bette. *Summer of My German Soldier.* Dial Books, 1973.

    An unlikely friendship between a Jewish girl and a German soldier during World War II marks the beginning of some shattering experiences for a twelve-year-old girl in Arkansas. A young girl searches for the strength to survive in a bitterly unhappy family.

R

Hunt, Irene. *Across Five Aprils.* Follett, 1965.

    In April, 1861, the Civil War became a reality for the Creighton family on their farm in southern Illinois. One by one the war pulled the able-bodied men away, leaving only the youngest, Jethro, to keep the farm going. The great war that ran across five Aprils is chronicled by the author.

E

	Type of entry	Culture

Hunter, Mollie. *You Never Knew Her As I Did.* Harper Junior Books, 1981. **R**

A young boy tries to help Mary, Queen of Scots, escape from her Scot captors in the mid-sixteenth century.

Kelly, Eric P. *Trumpeter of Krakow.* Macmillan, 1966. **C**

The author tells how the commemoration of an act of bravery and self-sacrifice in ancient Krakow saved the lives of a family two centuries later. This story of Poland is full of adventure and mystery.

O'Dell, Scott. *Carlota.* Houghton, 1977. **R H**

Raised to take the place of her dead brother, Carlota de Zubaran races her stallion through the California lowlands, dives into shark-infested waters searching for gold, and fights in the battles that rage between the Mexicans and the Americans. Yet, while Carlota thoroughly enjoys her freedom, she wants to be free to show feelings of tenderness and compassion as well. Her father thinks such feelings are shameful, so Carlota must defy him.

Perez, N. A. *One Special Year.* Houghton, 1985. **R**

A girl and her family live in turn-of-the-century upstate New York.

Rawlings, Marjorie Kinnen. *The Yearling.* Scribner, 1938. **C**

Young Jody Baxter lives a lonely life in the scrub forest of Florida until his parents unwillingly consent to his adopting an orphan fawn. The two become inseparable until the fawn destroys the meager crops. Jody then realizes that the situation offers no compromise. In the sacrifice of what he loves best, he leaves behind his own yearling days.

Rawls, Wilson. *Where the Red Fern Grows.* Bantam/Doubleday, 1961. **R**

Basing the story on his own boyhood in the Ozarks, the author tells a heartwarming tale of the love and loyalty between a boy and his two hunting hounds. Although the many coon-hunting scenes are presented from a hunter's viewpoint, this book is an action-packed favorite from beginning to end.

Richter, Hans Peter. *Friedrich.* Holt, 1969 (issued in 1961 in German as "Damals es Friedrich"). **R**

In chronological episodes a young boy tells about the fate of his Jewish friend, Friedrich, in Nazi Germany. Friedrich's life becomes a torment as his family is destroyed and he himself is forced into hiding, alone and in secrecy. This is an intense and unforgettable story of the persecution of the German Jews.

Sebestyen, Ouida. *Words by Heart.* Little, 1979. **R B**

Lena, a young black girl, is determined to excel and be accepted by a narrow-minded and ignorant community. As Lena and her family prove themselves, they are rewarded by violence, which brings death to her beloved father. Lena's courage to venture beyond fear makes the tale compelling and rewarding.

	Type of entry	Culture

Speare, Elizabeth. *The Witch of Blackbird Pond.* Houghton, 1958. **C**

A young girl, Kit Tyler, goes to live with her Puritan aunt in Wethersfield, Connecticut. It is 1687 and at Blackbird Pond she meets a witch and Nathaniel Eaton, the captain's son. The resulting witch-hunt and trial will hold any young reader's interest.

Sutcliff, Rosemary. *Song for a Dark Queen.* Crowell, 1979. **R**

This is the story of Boudicca, queen of the Iceni, in Roman Britain of the first century A.D. and of her unsuccessful struggle to free her people from brutal Roman rule.

Taylor, Mildred. *Roll of Thunder, Hear My Cry.* Dial Books, 1976; Bantam, 1978. **R** **B**

In this story, which is set in Mississippi during the 1930s, the Logan family is unforgettable in its determination to rise above the prejudices of that day. Cassie Logan, daughter of the family, finally understands why the land means so much to the independence of her black family.

Mystery

Alcock, Vivien. *Travelers by Night.* Delacorte, 1985. **C**

The circus is going out of business, and two circus children are going to be sent to live with relatives. Desperate to save an ancient elephant from slaughter, they kidnap the beast and commence their dangerous journey across England to a safari park.

Christie, Agatha. Selected novels. **R**

This British author of numerous mysteries, with intricate plots, provides easy reading and interesting characters.

Cross, Gillian. *On the Edge.* Holiday, 1985. **E**

Thirteen-year-old Liam (Tug) is an investigative reporter. When she antagonizes a terrorist group, Tug is kidnapped and undergoes brainwashing in an isolated cottage.

Doyle, Arthur Conan. *The Hound of the Baskervilles.* Dell, 1959. **R**

This case, based on a Devonshire legend, is a classic. The demonic howling of the hound calls Sherlock Holmes and Dr. Watson on an eerie adventure.

Hughes, Monica. *Devil on My Back.* Atheneum, 1985. **E**

This is a very contemporary novel, complete with computer, in which the hero, Tomi, discovers the very fine line between good and evil.

Hunter, Mollie. *The Thirteenth Member.* Harper Junior Books, 1971. **C**

Set in sixteenth-century Scotland, this is the story of a plot to murder King James I. Witchcraft is the weapon.

Sherlock Holmes Through Time and Space. Edited by Isaac Asimov. Bluejay Books, 1984. **C**

This collection of 15 short stories by well-known writers features Sherlock Holmes in science-fiction settings.

	Type of entry	Culture

Snyder, Zilpha K. *The Changeling*. Atheneum, 1970; Dell, 1986. — **R**

Flashbacks are used to tell the story of Martha and her long friendship with Ivy. Because Ivy claims to be the child of supernatural parents, who could expect her to be an ordinary teenager?

Mythology

Crosley-Holland, Keith. *The Norse Myths* (selections). Pantheon Books, 1980. — **R**

Norse tales are retold in a manner that captures the burlesque Norse humor and ferociousness.

Farmer, Penelope, and Chris Connor. *The Serpent's Teeth: The Story of Cadmus*. Harcourt, 1972. — **R**

The story of Cadmus's search for his sister Europa is retold in forceful fashion.

Highwater, Jamake. *Legend Days* (Plains). Hamlyn, 1969. — **R** **I**

Amana is gifted by the fox with the power of a warrior in her heart. These tales of the American Indians of the northern Great Plains are layered with symbolism and the supernatural.

Jataka Tales. Edited by Nancy De Roin. Houghton, 1975. — **R** **I**

These birth stories of famous Indians are 2,000 years old. The tales are full of humor as clever animals outwit each other.

Pinsent, John. *Greek Mythology*. Peter Bedrick Books, 1983. — **R**

Some unfamiliar as well as familiar Greek myths are retold and traced from their primitive development to more sophisticated versions.

Science Fiction and Fantasy

Bradbury, Ray. *Dandelion Wine*. Hart-Davis, 1957. — **C**

During one golden summer in 1928, twelve-year-old Douglas and his brother wander in and out of the lives of their elders. Douglas is sometimes aware and sometimes just having a wonderful time.

Christopher, John. *The White Mountains*. Macmillan, 1967. — **R**

In this first trilogy in a saga, the interplanetary Tripoda and Masters threaten all life on earth.

Cooper, Susan. *The Grey King*. Macmillan, 1975. — **C**

In this Arthurian fantasy the author describes the experiences of Will Stanton, Bran the sheep dog, and the ghostly grey foxes that are drawn together in an epic struggle of a world beyond time.

Harris, Geraldine. *The Seven Citadels* (series). Greenwillow, 1982. — **R**

In the first book in a series of fantasies, Prince of the Godborn is an emperor's son who sets out to free the mythical savior who is imprisoned by seven sorcerers.

Pierce, Meredith. *The Darkangel*. Little, 1982. — **R**

This is the first in a science-fiction trilogy about a young girl on the moon. She has a mysterious fate contained in a poem that she cannot interpret.

AS EVERY TEACHER KNOWS, MOTIVATION IS ONE OF THE KEYS TO LEARNING TO READ.

	Type of entry	Culture

Sleator, William. *Singularity.* Dutton, 1985.

R

Twin brothers, whose mother has just inherited a farmhouse, explore the grounds around the house and discover an unearthly secret: a passageway to another universe and a deadly force so great it could destroy the world.

Verne, Jules. *Journey to the Center of the Earth.* Dodd, 1984.

C

Explorers go down the funnel of a volcano in Iceland and are ejected near Stromboli in the Mediterranean. After a journey through the subterranean regions, they find animal and vegetable productions similar to those of past geological periods.

Short Stories

Connell, Richard. "The Most Dangerous Game," in *Tales of Fear and Frightening Phenomena.* Edited by Helen Hoke. Lodestar Books, 1982.

C

A world-renowned hunter becomes the prey of a sportsman who, bored pursuing wild game, selects the only animal capable of reason, a human being.

De Maupassant, Guy. *The Necklace.* Putnam, 1903.

C

The heroine borrows a diamond necklace to wear at a party and loses it. Years of hard work are required to pay for the necklace, which turns out to be a fake. This is a classic tale of irony.

Irving, Washington. *The Legend of Sleepy Hollow.* Watts, 1966.

C

This story, set in the Hudson River Valley, is about the superstitious schoolmaster Ichabod Crane, who is frightened away from a promising courtship after an encounter with the legendary headless horseman.

Irving, Washington. *Rip Van Winkle.* Macmillan, 1963.

C

Rip Van Winkle has a 20-year-long nap after he drinks from a keg offered by a dwarf. He returns to the town and learns that his wife is dead, his daughter is married, and the king's portrait has been replaced by one of George Washington.

Jacobs, W. W. "The Monkey's Paw," in *The Dark Company: The Ten Greatest Ghost Stories.* Edited by Lincoln Child. St. Martin's Press, 1984.

C

In this well-known story, the author takes the fairy-tale theme of *The Three Wishes* and gives it a sinister twist with a new light.

Keyes, Daniel. *Flowers for Algernon.* Harcourt, 1966.

C

A surgeon and a psychologist develop a dramatic way to increase the intelligence of a mentally retarded man, but the results are short-lived.

Kipling, Rudyard. *The Jungle Book.* Grosset and Dunlap, 1950.

C

This is a collection of stories from India about the jungle life of Mowgli, a boy adopted and nurtured by a wolf pack. Bagheera the panther and Baloo the bear prove to be apt teachers for the young boy

	Type of entry	Culture

Kipling, Rudyard. *Just So Stories.* Doubleday, 1902.   **C**

    This book contains Kipling's original explanations of how the tiger got its spots, the elephant, its trunk, and other equally interesting questions.

Kipling, Rudyard. *Rikki-Tikki-Tavi.* Children's Press, 1982.   **C**

    This book contains more stories of the Indian jungle creatures, including the mongoose, the white seal, and other animal personalities.

Poe, Edgar Allan. "The Cask of Amontillado," in *Great Short Works of Edgar Allan Poe.* Edited by J. R. Thompson. Harper and Row, 1970.   **C**

    Details of a 55-year-old crime of revenge are gloatingly revealed by the murderer.

Poe, Edgar Allan. "The Tell-Tale Heart," in *Great Short Works of Edgar Allan Poe.* Harper and Row, 1970.   **C**

    After cleverly concealing the body, a murderer confesses his crime, believing he is betrayed by the beating of the victim's heart.

Traven, B. "Assembly Line," in *The Night Visitor and Other Stories.* Hill and Wang, 1966.   **C** **H**

    An American in Mexico, encountering an Indian peasant making exquisite little straw baskets, hopes to make a fortune by persuading him to increase his output and is confounded by the artist's refusal to compromise his "unsung poems."

Plays

Childress, Alice. *When the Rattlesnake Sounds: A Play About Harriet Tubman.* Coward, 1975.   **C**

    This play covers one year in the life of Harriet Tubman, who, despite a $40,000 reward being offered for her capture, still furthers the cause of abolition and the work of the Underground Railroad.

Gibson, William. *The Miracle Worker.* Knopf, 1957.   **C**

    This is a dramatization of the conflict between the young Helen Keller and her teacher, Anne Sullivan. The conflict ends when Helen discovers the language of the blind and deaf.

Giraudoux, Jean. *Apollo of Bellac,* in *Four Plays,* Vol. 1. Hill and Wang, 1958.   **R**

    In this play a shabby unprepossessing vagabond poet dreams of the great things he will do, but he never does anything.

Gonzales, Gloria. *Gaucho.* Knopf, 1977.   **R** **H**

    A Puerto Rican boy living in New York is torn between returning to his native island or exploring the opportunities and hope offered by his new city home.

Osborn, Paul. *On Borrowed Time.* Knopf, 1938.   **R**

    An old man plots to outwit death to avoid having his grandson brought up by an unpleasant aunt. The comedy is based on the novel by Lawrence Edward Watkin.

	Type of entry	Culture

Serling Rod. ***Monsters Are Due On Maple Street.*** Houghton (Cross-currents Action Series), n.d. — **C**

Inexplicable occurrences convince the residents of Maple Street that one of their neighbors is an alien from another planet. This originally was a script for a *Twilight Zone* episode on television.

Sherwood, Robert. ***Abe Lincoln in Illinois*** (a play in 12 scenes). Scribner, 1939. — **C**

This play deals with the life of Lincoln up to his election to the presidency. The dialogue contains selections from a number of Lincoln's own speeches and writings.

INDEX OF AUTHORS

Mowat, Farley 100
Munari, Bruno 69
Musgrove, Margaret 6
Myers, Walter D. 103

N

Nance, John 44
Nesbit, Edith 80
Ness, Evaline 33
Neville, Emily C. 86
Newlon, Clarke 49
Newman, Deborah 54
Nguyen, Lan 58, 75
Nhuong, Huynh Quang 49
Noble, Trinka H. 80
Norton, Mary 20
Nye, Robert 101

O

O'Brien, Robert C. 20
O'Dell, Scott 38, 86, 89, 99, 105
O'Neill, Mary 27
Orlev, Uri 38
Osborn, Paul 109

P

Pace, Mildred 44
Parish, Peggy 80
Paterson, Katherine 33, 103
Patterson, Francine 44
Paul, Paula G. 86
Paz, Marcela 61
Peck, Richard 38
Peck, Robert N. 100
Peet, Bill 20, 81
Pellicer Lopez, Carlos 61
Perez, N. A. 105
Perrault, Charles 57
Petry, Ann 100
Pierce, Meredith 107
Pinsent, John 107
Piper, Watty 20
Place, Marian T. 96
Plotz, Helen (Ed.) 25
Poe, Edgar Allan 109
Politi, Leo 6, 33, 44, 75, 86
Pomerantz, Charlotte 27
Potter, Beatrix 6
Prelutsky, Jack 27, 83
Preston, Carol 54
Price, Christine 44
Provensen, Alice, and Martin
  Provensen 49
Proysen, Alf 57
Pushkin, Alexander 58
Pyle, Howard 101
Pyle, Howard (Ed.) 14

Q

Quackenbush, Robert 49

R

Raboff, Ernest 50
Ransome, Arthur 75
Raskin, Ellen 69, 86
Rawlings, Marjorie K. 105
Rawls, Wilson 34, 105
Reeves, James 75
Reiss, Johanna 50
Reiss, John J. 69
Rey, Hans A. 69
Richter, Hans P. 105
Roberts, Naurice 50
Robinson, Barbara 86
Rockwell, Anne 44, 50
Rockwell, Thomas 54
Rockwood, Joyce 89
Rodgers, Mary 20
Rohmer, Harriet 59
Roland, Donna 14
Rosario, Idalia 6
Rounds, Glen 14
Roxlo, Conrado Nale 60
Rudeen, Kenneth 50

S

Sachs, Marilyn 34, 86, 89
Saiki, Patsy S. 89
Sandburg, Carl 27, 100
Sandoz, Mari 89
Santa Elena, Antonio E. 89
Santrey, Laurence 96
Sattler, Helen R. 44
Sawyer, Ruth 89
Schaaf, Peter 93
Schlesinger, Sarah 52
Schoolcraft, Henry R. (Ed.) 71
Schultz de Mantovani, Fryda 59
Schweitzer, Byrd B. 6, 89
Scott, Ann H. 6
Scott, Jack D. 44, 93
Sebestyen, Ouida 105
Selden, George 21
Selsam, Millicent E. 44, 45, 93
Selsam, Millicent E., and Jerome
  Wexler 93
Sendak, Maurice 21, 69, 83
Serling, Rod 110
Seuss, Dr. 21, 69, 81
Sewell, Helen, and Thomas
  Bulfinch 75
Shecter, Ben 69
Sherwood, Robert 110
Shub, Elizabeth 39
Shulevitz, Uri 14, 75

INDEX OF TITLES

N

O

P

PUBLICATIONS AVAILABLE FROM THE DEPARTMENT OF EDUCATION

This publication is one of over 650 that are available from the California State Department of Education. Some of the more recent publications or those most widely used are the following:

ISBN	Title (Date of publication)	Price
0-8011-0271-5	Academic Honesty (1986)	$2.50
0-8011-0722-9	Accounting Procedures for Student Organizations (1988)	3.75
0-8011-0272-3	Administration of Maintenance and Operations in California School Districts (1986)	6.75
0-8011-0216-2	Bilingual-Crosscultural Teacher Aides: A Resource Guide (1984)	3.50
0-8011-0238-3	Boating the Right Way (1985)	4.00
0-8011-0275-8	California Dropouts: A Status Report (1986)	2.50
0-8011-0707-5	California Private School Directory, 1987-88 (1987)	14.00
0-8011-0724-5	California Public School Directory (1988)	14.00
0-8011-0715-6	California Women: Activities Guide, K—12 (1988)	3.50
0-8011-0488-2	Caught in the Middle: Educational Reform for Young Adolescents in California Public Schools (1987)	5.00
0-8011-0241-3	Computer Applications Planning (1985)	5.00
0-8011-0242-1	Computers in Education: Goals and Content (1985)	2.50
0-8011-0749-0	Educational Software Preview Guide, 1988-89 (1988)	2.00
0-8011-0489-0	Effective Practices in Achieving Compensatory Education-Funded Schools II (1987)	5.00
0-8011-0041-0	English-Language Arts Framework for California Public Schools (1987)	3.00
0-8011-0731-8	English-Language Arts Model Curriculum Guide, K—8 (1988)	3.00
0-8011-0710-5	Family Life/Sex Education Guidelines (1987)	4.00
0-8011-0744-4	From Vision to Reality: California Educational Reform—Annual Report, 1987 (1988)	3.00
0-8011-0289-8	Handbook for Physical Education (1986)	4.50
0-8011-0249-9	Handbook for Planning an Effective Foreign Language Program (1985)	3.50
0-8011-0320-7	Handbook for Planning an Effective Literature Program (1987)	3.00
0-8011-0179-4	Handbook for Planning an Effective Mathematics Program (1982)	2.00
0-8011-0290-1	Handbook for Planning an Effective Writing Program (1986)	2.50
0-8011-0224-3	Handbook for Teaching Cantonese-Speaking Students (1984)	4.50
0-8011-0680-X	Handbook for Teaching Japanese-Speaking Students (1987)	4.50
0-8011-0291-X	Handbook for Teaching Pilipino-Speaking Students (1986)	4.50
0-8011-0204-9	Handbook for Teaching Portuguese-Speaking Students (1983)	4.50
0-8011-0250-2	Handbook on California Education for Language Minority Parents— Chinese/English Edition (1985)	3.25*
0-8011-0737-7	Here They Come: Ready or Not—Report of the School Readiness Task Force (1988)	2.00
0-8011-0712-1	History-Social Science Framework for California Public Schools (1988)	6.00
0-8011-0227-8	Individual Learning Programs for Limited-English-Proficient Students (1984)	3.50
0-8011-0466-1	Instructional Patterns: Curriculum for Parenthood Education (1985)	12.00
0-8011-0208-1	Manual of First-Aid Practices for School Bus Drivers (1983)	1.75
0-8011-0209-X	Martin Luther King, Jr., 1929—1968 (1983)	3.25
0-8011-0358-4	Mathematics Framework for California Public Schools (1985)	3.00
0-8011-0664-8	Mathematics Model Curriculum Guide, K—8 (1987)	2.75
0-8011-0685-0	Microcomputers for Use in School District Administration (1987)	9.00
0-8011-0725-3	Model Curriculum for Human Rights and Genocide (1988)	3.25
0-8011-0252-9	Model Curriculum Standards: Grades 9—12 (1985)	5.50
0-8011-0229-4	Nutrition Education—Choose Well, Be Well: A Curriculum Guide for Junior High School (1984)	8.00
0-8011-0228-6	Nutrition Education—Choose Well, Be Well: A Curriculum Guide for High School (1984)	8.00
0-8011-0182-4	Nutrition Education—Choose Well, Be Well: A Curriculum Guide for Preschool and Kindergarten (1982)	8.00
0-8011-0183-2	Nutrition Education—Choose Well, Be Well: A Curriculum Guide for the Primary Grades (1982)	8.00

*The following editions are also available, at the same price: Armenian/English, Cambodian/English, Hmong/English, Japanese/English, Korean/English, Laotian/English, Pilipino/English, Samoan/English, Spanish/English, and Vietnamese/English.

ISBN	Title (Date of publication)	Price
0-8011-0184-0	Nutrition Education—Choose Well, Be Well: A Curriculum Guide for the Upper Elementary Grades (1982)	$8.00
0-8011-0230-8	Nutrition Education—Choose Well, Be Well: A Resource Manual for Parent and Community Involvement in Nutrition Education Programs (1984)	4.50
0-8011-0185-9	Nutrition Education—Choose Well, Be Well: A Resource Manual for Preschool, Kindergarten, and Elementary Teachers (1982)	2.25
0-8011-0303-7	A Parent's Handbook on California Education (1986)	3.25
0-8011-0305-3	Paths Through High School: A California Curriculum Study (1987)	4.00
0-8011-0671-0	Practical Ideas for Teaching Writing as a Process (1987)	6.00
0-8011-0309-6	Program Guidelines for Hearing Impaired Individuals (1986)	6.00
0-8011-0258-8	Program Guidelines for Severely Orthopedically Impaired Individuals (1985)	6.00
0-8011-0684-2	Program Guidelines for Visually Impaired Individuals (1987)	6.00
0-8011-0213-8	Raising Expectations: Model Graduation Requirements (1983)	2.75
0-8011-0311-8	Recommended Readings in Literature, K—8 (1986)	2.25
0-8011-0745-8	Recommended Readings in Literature, K—8, Annotated Edition (1988)	4.50
0-8011-0214-6	School Attendance Improvement: A Blueprint for Action (1983)	2.75
0-8011-0189-1	Science Education for the 1980s (1982)	2.50
0-8011-0339-8	Science Framework for California Public Schools (1978)	3.00
0-8011-0354-1	Science Framework Addendum (1984)	3.00
0-8011-0665-6	Science Model Curriculum Guide, K—8 (1987)	3.25
0-8011-0668-0	Science Safety Handbook for California High Schools (1987)	8.75
0-8011-0677-X	Secondary Textbook Review: General Mathematics (1987)	6.50
0-8011-0691-5	Selected Financial and Related Data for California Public Schools (1987)	3.00
0-8011-0265-0	Standards for Scoliosis Screening in California Public Schools (1985)	2.50
0-8011-0486-6	Statement on Preparation in Natural Science Expected of Entering Freshmen (1986)	2.50
0-8011-0318-5	Students' Rights and Responsibilities Handbook (1986)	2.75
0-8011-0234-0	Studies on Immersion Education: A Collection for U.S. Educators (1984)	5.00
0-8011-0682-6	Suicide Prevention Program for California Public Schools (1987)	8.00
0-8011-0739-3	Survey of Academic Skills, Grade 8: Rationale and Content for Science (1988)	2.50
0-8011-0192-1	Trash Monster Environmental Education Kit (for grade six)	23.00
0-8011-0236-7	University and College Opportunities Handbook (1984)	3.25
0-8011-0344-4	Visual and Performing Arts Framework for California Public Schools (1982)	3.25
0-8011-0237-5	Wet 'n' Safe: Water and Boating Safety, Grades 4—6 (1983)	2.50
0-8011-0194-8	Wizard of Waste Environmental Education Kit (for grade three)	20.00
0-8011-0670-2	Work Experience Education Instructional Guide (1987)	12.50
0-8011-0464-5	Work Permit Handbook (1985)	6.00
0-8011-0736-9	Writing Assessment Handbook: Grade 12 (1987)	12.00
0-8011-0686-9	Year-round Education: Year-round Opportunities—A Study of Year-round Education in California (1987)	5.00
0-8011-0270-7	Young and Old Together: A Resource Directory of Intergenerational Resources (1986)	3.00

Orders should be directed to:

California State Department of Education
P.O. Box 271
Sacramento, CA 95802-0271

Please include the International Standard Book Number (ISBN) for each title ordered.

Remittance or purchase order must accompany order. Purchase orders without checks are accepted only from governmental agencies. Sales tax should be added to all orders from California purchasers.

A complete list of publications available from the Department, including apprenticeship instructional materials, may be obtained by writing to the address listed above or by calling (916) 445-1260.

ORDER FORM

Date _____

Name _____

Address _____

_____
City   State   ZIP code

Title and date of publication	ISBN	Number of copies	Price per copy	Total
Recommended Readings in Literature, Annotated Edition (1988)	0-8011-0745-8		**$4.50**	

Make checks payable to:
California State Department of Education

California residents add sales tax $ _____

Total amount $ _____

Mail to:
California State Department of Education
P.O. Box 271
Sacramento, CA 95802-0271

NOTE: Remittance or purchase order must accompany order. Purchase orders without checks are accepted only from governmental agencies.

86-193 (03-0492) 81704-300 7-88 20M